The
Young and Fair

A PLAY

by

N. RICHARD NASH

DRAMATISTS
PLAY SERVICE · INC.
NEW YORK

For
JERRY UCHIN

THE PLACE

The action of the play takes place in the Brook Valley Academy, not far from Boston.

In the old days, some forty years ago, the school used to be known as a Seminary for Young Women. With a change in fashion, it was re-named a Finishing School. Today it's a junior college and is called an Academy. Whatever its title, the school itself—its traditions, its ideals, its objectives—has remained quite unchanged. To quote the catalogue, sent on request to eligible girls between the ages of sixteen and twenty:

"Brook Valley Academy, situated in one of Boston's most charming suburbs, combines the advantages of graceful country life and the cultural activities of Boston. Here, well-born young women are offered all opportunity to steep themselves in the amenities of discriminating living. For the preparatory school graduate who is desirous of continuing her education, but who is hesitant about taking up the rigors of a four-year college, Brook Valley is ideal. Because here—in two years—she may achieve a terminal education which will equip her to step gracefully into her position in her cultivated sphere. . . ."

For all the emphasis on grace and elegance and finesse, Brook Valley does not neglect its academic standards. In educational circles, its students are highly credited—and those of its graduates who do desire to take two more years of college, at Bryn Mawr or Vassar or Wellesley, acquit themselves meritoriously in the senior colleges.

There are three buildings. Fairchild Hall was built first and is the main building. Then came Cantry House, named after the founder and present owner of Brook Valley; finally, Weatherby. The action of the play takes place in Fairchild Hall—in its office, in one of its bedrooms and in the main hallway.

. . . The time of the play is now . . .

THE SCENE

This is a one-set play.

However, the set is not a conventional one and is not meant to convey the place with any slavish fidelity to realism.

The stage is to be so divided as to give the illusion of three rooms; rather, three playing areas. These are:

Left stage, a corner of Fran Morritt's office.

Right stage, a section of Patty Morritt's bedroom.

Center stage—connecting the two—a kind of wedge-shaped area which is to designate the Main Hall. This Main Hall should have a stairway which turns out of sight behind the back wall of Patty's bedroom. And it should be so designed as to give the illusion of spilling out (upstage) upon a larger, more open area behind the stairway to the right and behind the wall of Fran's office to the left.

The whole back wall of the stage, behind everything—functioning almost like a cyclorama—should be some formalized or conventionalized treatment of great college windows in the typical "American Gothic" tradition of many American campuses.

Everything visible should set a tone of authentic and genteel good taste.

Put to practical use, this set should function in the following way:

At certain times during the play—for short periods—the entire set is illuminated so that the audience is witness to action going on in all three places simultaneously. Thus we can see the school at work—Fran in her office; activity in Patty's room; the going and coming of girls, the laughter and gossip, in the Main Hall.

For the most part, however, only one of these three areas will be alight at a single time. While a particular scene is being played in one of the three areas, the rest of the stage is, generally speaking, in darkness. At its termination, the next playing area is illuminated and the last one is in darkness. For example, in the second act, when Scene Two is being played, only the bedroom is alight; when it is over, the bedroom darkens and the office lights up for Scene Three.

Such a production scheme offers many opportunities. Possibly the most important of these is the fact that a fluidity and high pace of action are sustained through the medium of living, moving light.

Secondly, it is possible through this plan to play *two* actions— a major one and a subordinate one—at the same time. Thus, while Dru and Lee are in the bedroom discussing a matter that vitally concerns Patty, the latter is visible downstairs in the Main Hall waiting for Lee. Here is a chance to light up the bedroom for the major action and simultaneously reveal Patty in the half-light of the Main Hall. We can see Patty's impatience while she is waiting for Lee to come downstairs; we notice Patty look at her watch, debating whether to go up the stairs to fetch Lee; we see her go to the stairs, etc. This double-decker action, not feasible if the play is done conventionally, can add color and suspense to many moments of playing.

Thirdly, this scheme of production carries out more potently than would be possible if there were scenery to shift, the mounting climax which is the very mechanism of the play.

One word more: there are numberless instances throughout the play when this extra-dimensional decor can be resourcefully put to use. I have not indicated these instances in the script but have left them to the invention of the director.

THE YOUNG AND FAIR *was produced in New York City at the Fulton Theatre where it opened on Monday, November 22, 1948. The following is a copy of the program:*

VINTON FREEDLEY
(in association with RICHARD W. KRAKEUR)

PRESENTS

THE YOUNG AND FAIR

by N. Richard Nash
Directed by Harold Clurman
Setting by Paul Morrison
Costumes by Eleanor Goldsmith

CAST

(In the order of their appearance)

EMMY FOSTER	FRIEDA ALTMAN
FRANCES MORRITT	MERCEDES MCCAMBRIDGE
PATTY MORRITT	PATRICIA KIRKLAND
SARA CANTRY	FRANCES STARR
LAURA CANTRY	BETTY MORRISSEY
LEE BARRON	LOIS WHEELER
SELMA KEENEY	LENKA PETERSON
NANCY GEAR	JULIE HARRIS
MIL CHEAVER	FRANCES FREEMAN
DRUCILLA ELDRIDGE	DOE AVEDON
MARY LOUISE	PATRICIA BOUCHARD
SYLVIA	PEGGY O'CONNOR
SALLY	ANN SORG
HELEN	VICKI CARLSON
GLORIA	RITA GAM
SUE	ANN MURPHY
MATHILDA	ELAINE BRADFORD
BOOTS MCGREGOR	SALLY MOFFET
GEORGETTA	MARY LOU PHELAN
PAULINE	LEE TRUHILL
CAROL	BETTE STANLEY

The action of the play takes place in the Brook Valley Academy, a girls' Junior College not far from Boston.

TIME: THE PRESENT

ACT I.

Scene 1. Miss Cantry's Office in Fairchild Hall. An afternoon in late September.

Scene 2. A Bedroom in Fairchild Hall. Immediately following.

Scene 3. The Lounge in Fairchild Hall. Friday afternoon, a week later.

ACT II.

Scene 1. The Office. The following afternoon.

Scene 2. The Bedroom. Immediately after.

Scene 3. The Office. Later, the same afternoon.

ACT III.

Scene 1. The Bedroom. An hour later.

Scene 2. The Office. A half hour later.

ACT I

Scene 1

When the curtain rises the stage is in darkness except for the light coming through the three college windows designed in the typical American Gothic tradition of many eastern campuses. For a moment we see nothing indoors, but we do get a glimpse, through the windows, of a well-landscaped campus, still green in the mid-afternoon sunlight of late September. From somewhere comes the sound of mellifluous class bells. [*These are heard intermittently throughout the play.*] *The bells now are the cue for the light to come up, sharp and clear, on—*

The Office

The office in Fairchild Hall is a businesslike room with desk and filing cabinet, but ingenuity has been strained to soften its official nature. The chairs are tastefully upholstered; the chintzy drapes and frills are designed to make the room charmingly feminine and colorful.

EMMY FOSTER, *a thin-faced, middle-aged maid, opens the door and shows* FRANCES *and* PATTY MORRITT *into the room . . .* FRANCES *is nearing thirty. The most immediate feeling we get about her is that she is well-born. Though she is a serious person, there is nothing solemn about her. As a matter of fact, she likes to laugh, which she does in a quiet, mental kind of way. Besides being fond of* PATTY, *her sixteen-year-old sister,* FRANCES *enjoys the girl.* PATTY, *for her part, enjoys everything. She is going through a period when—learning to think—she enjoys that too, immensely. An impetuous girl with warm impulses.*

EMMY. I'll tell Miss Cantry you're here. What name again, please?

FRAN. Morritt. Patricia and Frances Morritt. (EMMY *goes out.* FRAN *moves about, surveying the room in sentimental remembrance*)

PATTY. Is it the way you remembered it?

FRAN. (*Warmly*) Exactly. The drapes have changed—but everything else—just as it was nine years ago. The same picture of Martha Washington and—look—(*She goes to the desk on which: a silver cup, a water pitcher and a bottle of sodamints*)—Miss Cantry's silver cup, her water pitcher and her bicarbonate of soda tablets. Nothing's changed.

PATTY. Not even her digestion. (*They both laugh quietly. The class bells ring softly*)

FRAN. The same old class bells! It's lovely—everything's so lovely. I'd better stop this or I'll weep.

PATTY. Fran, do all junior colleges look like this? (*At window—touching the drape*) I mean, half college and half chintz?

FRAN. The chintz is camouflage—so you won't get nervous.

PATTY. Who's nervous?

FRAN. Me. I'm shaking like a leaf.

PATTY. Don't you worry, Fran—you'll get the job. After all, you're an alumna—and Miss Cantry likes you. It's in the bag.

FRAN. I hope so, Dumpling.

PATTY. Fran, please—when you're a teacher and I'm a student—don't call me Dumpling. In college they call girls Miss, don't they? Kind of nice. (*She giggles*) But awfully silly.

FRAN. Baby, don't rattle.

PATTY. I promise when you're talking to Miss Cantry, I won't open my mouth.

FRAN. She'll think you're a deaf mute. And sometimes *I* think not a bad idea. (PATTY *giggles again*) Sh—Patty.

PATTY. Fran, you're so jumpy.

FRAN. I'm scared, Pat. Every decent job I've applied for—no soap. I've just got to land this one.

PATTY. (*Soberly*) You wouldn't be nearly so worried if you didn't have my dead weight to carry.

FRAN. Patty, I *need* this job—for myself. I want to be here again —to work here—live here. And I want you with me.

PATTY. Yes—we've got to stay together—we've got to! (*Sound of footsteps in the hall*)

FRAN. Here comes somebody.

PATTY. Good luck—oh, good luck! (*The door opens and* MISS CANTRY *enters.* SARA CANTRY *is in her early sixties. But her years and her almost-white hair belie her real energies: Mental energy—quick, keen, shrewd; nervous energy—sensitive, anxious, high-strung. But her most manifest quality is her studied, captivating charm*)

CANTRY. Frances! Frances Morritt! Oh, it's been so long, my dear!

FRAN. (*As they embrace*) Miss Cantry! It's wonderful to see you again!

CANTRY. Nearly ten years, isn't it! . . . And don't tell me this is that baby sister. Patricia, isn't it?

PATTY. That's right.

CANTRY. (*Warmly*) Welcome to Brook Valley, both of you. I was so distressed not to have seen you last week. But I was away for a few days, resting up before the opening of school. However, I'm glad you saw Miss Van Zandt. Frances, she was quite taken by you—as I told her she would be.

FRAN. She was very kind.

CANTRY. We'll miss her here. I hope you'll make up for her loss—and I'm sure you will. Please sit down. Would you like some tea—or a Coca Cola? (*She reaches over to the desk and rings a bell*)

FRAN. No, thank you.

CANTRY. You won't mind if I do, will you? The girls have been coming in all day and I've said, "Have you had a nice summer?" so often that my throat is absolutely raw. (*Gently*) Frances, Miss Van Zandt told me about your father's death. I'm very sorry. (FRAN *whispers her thanks.* CANTRY *studies her and continues, fondly*) My dear, you haven't changed. Essentially, I mean, you're as you were. And I'm so glad.

FRAN. Thank you. I was going to say the same about you—and Brook Valley.

CANTRY. (*With a laugh*) Oh, we change with the years. The poplar trees grow taller, the girls seem younger and the board of trustees gets more and more devilish.

FRAN. Are those trustees still bedevilling you?

CANTRY. Yes, but I'll tell you a secret. Any day now we're going to be endowed! Then we'll pay those trustees off—and live in peace again.

FRAN. How wonderful! Who's the benefactor?

CANTRY. I daren't tell you that—it's still in the deep, dark stage. But I really think it'll come through!

FRAN. I can't tell you how happy I am for you. I've always felt the school *should* be endowed.

CANTRY. Exactly—it should be! After all, we've established something quite special and fine here. And what a struggle it's been! Driving to keep up enrollment—fighting through two depressions—! And now—forty years after I began—it's about to come!

(EMMY *enters*) Oh, Emmy. Would you bring me some iced tea, please. And you won't forget the lime this time, will you?

EMMY. No, Miss Cantry. (*She goes out and* CANTRY *continues*)

CANTRY. Yes, forty years. And here I am—still a crabby old spinster—and I love it! (*She laughs and they join her. Then, focusing on* FRAN) Frances, I suppose Miss Van Zandt explained about the position. It's a good deal more than merely teaching English, you know.

FRAN. Yes, she said something about my being personnel director.

CANTRY. I'm trying to visualize you in her place—you're so much younger.

FRAN. I can look a great deal older. (*More lightly*) As a matter of fact, I generally do. I'm so sorry I'm having such a good day.

CANTRY. Gracious, don't apologize for good days—pray for them! I do—but it gets me nowhere . . . I don't suppose youth is a disadvantage in a personnel director . . . Still . . . (PATTY, *apprehensive about the doubt in* CANTRY's *voice, speaks up impulsively:*)

PATTY. Fran is a wonderful personnel director. She's all the director I've got.

CANTRY. (*Charmingly*) And she's done an excellent job with you, Patricia.

PATTY. Besides, Fran has been around quite a lot. She's been in nearly every capital in South America.

FRAN. That's a slight exaggeration, but Patty and I did travel a good deal with my father.

CANTRY. Oh, yes. He was with the State Department, wasn't he? Some sort of ambassador . . . ?

FRAN. Nothing so grand as that—he was just an undersecretary.

CANTRY. Let me see now—it was Brazil, wasn't it?

FRAN. Yes, his last post was in Rio de Janeiro.

CANTRY. Frances, forgive my asking this but—when your father died I assume he left things financially a little uncertain for you . . . ?

FRAN. Miss Cantry, there's no uncertainty about it. We're broke. (*Then, wryly*) I'm afraid I'm a dreadful anachronism—one of the genteel poor. I haven't been trained to earn a living—and I need a position badly.

CANTRY. You're sure you would be happy teaching?

FRAN. Yes, quite sure. And it's the one thing I'd feel confident in doing. That may sound presumptuous—

CANTRY. Not at all.

FRAN. I suppose I *could* get some kind of typing job or go into a department store . . .

CANTRY. Heavens, that would be just the wrong thing for you— and what would you do with Patricia?

FRAN. That's just it. I'd hate to toss her out on her own—into a dreary job somewhere. Not yet—not till she's a bit tougher.

PATTY. I'm tougher than you think, Fran—I'm not an infant.

FRAN. (*Ignoring her*) I don't know what I'd do about her education. She's ready for college—and she's aching to go. But I don't see how we can manage. Point is, I want her to get at least as much as I've had!

CANTRY. (*Warmly*) You're the same, same Frances.

FRAN. (*Encouraged. With added intensity*) Miss Cantry, I don't care how little you pay me. Just our board and lodging and

6

Patty's tuition. Patty can be educated in the best place I know. And I'd be at work—doing what I want to do in the place I want to be.

CANTRY. Have you applied at any other schools?

FRAN. (*Openly*) Yes, I have. Selfridge Hall, Willowcrest—a half dozen of them. (*With a rueful smile*) They all want qualifications. I haven't got—a master's degree, years of experience . . . Everybody turned me down.

CANTRY. Why in heavens name didn't you come here first?

FRAN. Well . . . I know you're fond of me. I didn't want to presume on your affection—not until it was the last resort . . . This is it.

(*A knock at the door.* LAURA CANRTY, MISS CANTRY's *niece, half enters.* LAURA *is about thirty-five and unmarried. Her frustration hides behind her spirituelle manner, behind her breathless, frightened voice. She is tremulously subservient to her aunt*)

CANTRY. Come in, Laura. This is my niece, also a Cantry. Miss Morritt—and Miss Morritt.

FRAN. How do you do.

CANTRY. My niece is on the faculty. Gives a splendid course in Art Appreciation. I myself occasionally steal in to listen.

LAURA. (*To* FRAN) I feel as if I already know you. Auntie Sara has spoken of you so often . . . And every year or so there was a letter from you. Such charming letters . . .

FRAN. Thank you.

LAURA. Your last one came from Montevideo. It was a lovely letter—long and newsy. Do you remember it?

CANTRY. Nonsense, Laura. Travellers never recall their letters —only we stay-at-homes do.

FRAN. But I do remember that one. I recall the very day I posted it . . . April 12, 1945.

CANTRY. How odd that you should remember the exact date.

FRAN. That day . . . I was in a large post office in Montevideo. I had just dropped your letter in the box when a crowd gathered at the telegraph window. In the middle of the crowd there was a young man. I can still remember his voice, crying "Muerto! Muerto!" I've never seen such bereavement. He was ripping the buttons off his coat, crying "Muerto." . . . That's how I heard the news of President Roosevelt's death. . . .

CANTRY. (*After a moment*) What an unfortunate memory! . . . But, Frances, your family wasn't exactly pro-Roosevelt, was it?

FRAN. No, but we didn't cheer when he died.

CANTRY. Why, of course you didn't.

PATTY. (*Impulsively*) Me! I wept like a baby! (CANTRY *stiffens almost imperceptibly. It is not immediately clear whether her reaction is to what* PATTY *said—or to* PATTY's *impulsive manner of saying it . . .* FRAN *sees* CANTRY's *reaction and withdraws a bit*)

CANTRY. Really, Patricia? (*To* FRAN, *with a smile*) How about you, Frances? Did you weep?

FRAN. (*Cautiously*) Miss Cantry, I was a little girl when President Harding died. I wept because he was our president. I wept again when Roosevelt died . . . for the same reason.

CANTRY. I'm so glad you put it that way . . . It's precisely what I was driving at. You know Brook Valley. You can appreciate how awkward . . .

FRAN. I understand.

CANTRY. (*With a new surge of charm*) You know, for an instant I had the uneasy feeling we were on the verge of talking politics.

FRAN. Miss Cantry, my father used to say that a career man in the State Department must have no politics. I'm like my father: no politics.

CANTRY. Excellent! Precisely my sentiments. And they're sound sentiments for a place like Brook Valley. (*She pauses*) Frances, with a little experience I'm sure you could handle the English courses. But my first concern is the personnel work.

FRAN. Of course.

CANTRY. There's just one more question I want to ask—(*With an affable smile*) This is a dreadful inquisition for you.

FRAN. Not at all.

CANTRY. It's simply this. Do you remember an old motto we used to have? Heavens, I think your own class invented it!

FRAN. Enjoy Good Fortune with Good Taste. (*They both laugh*)

CANTRY. I know how juvenile it sounds—but I've always rather liked that little catch-phrase. Now tell me: what do you understand that motto to mean?

FRAN. Well, I—ten years ago I'd have had a ready answer.

LAURA. Perhaps I can help you out. I think Auntie Sara wants to know how you could correlate your work with that motto. Is that it?

CANTRY. Something like that.

LAURA (*Encouraged to go on*) For example, in my work it's quite simple. Let me see now—good taste—(*She is happy as a child who is given the opportunity to recite a lesson well learned. Her voice goes spirituelle*) Teaching Art Appreciation, I can show my girls how spiritual their lives can become if they will open their eyes to the masterpieces of Art. I can show them how they can become One with Michaelangelo, da Vinci, Botticelli. With good taste—

CANTRY. Excuse me, Laura. Good taste is only half the motto. It was the other half—the good fortune—(*Smiling but serious*) Frances, our girls are children of good fortune. We must remember that. And accept it—without prejudice. Now we all try to be quite liberal here without pulling and tearing at sacred institutions, but . . . My dear, if I say any more I'll be putting words in your mouth.

FRAN. Miss Cantry, if you want to know whether I'd fit in here again as I did once, I can only give you a character reference. You know where I came from—you knew my family—you must surely know me. I love this place—I spent the two happiest years of my life here, and—believe me—I want nothing changed. (CANTRY *flashes her a radiant smile. Then, quite moved, she rises*)

CANTRY. Frances, you have completely answered my question. Thank you—and welcome home! And welcome to you, Patricia. (FRAN *rises*) We'll talk about your duties a little later, when you're settled.

FRAN. (*Moved*) Miss Cantry, I can't tell you how much—

CANTRY. Please don't try. Truth to tell, I had my heart set on engaging you even before I set foot in this room. If something had gone amiss, I'd have been more disappointed than you! (*They all laugh*) Oh, yes—money. There'll be room and board for both of you—and Patricia's education without charge. In addition—let me see—two thousand dollars a year.

FRAN. (*Overcome*) Miss Cantry—I—it's so much more than I expected—

CANTRY. If I'm paying you a little extra it's for the extra pleasure of having you here.

FRAN. Thank you. Thank you very much. (FRAN *turns away to conceal how touched she is. But* PATTY *is unashamedly teary-eyed. She finds her handkerchief and honks into it noisily . . . Everybody laughs.*)

CANTRY. Incidentally, you can use my office so we can work together for a little while. Your bedroom's in the faculty wing in Cantry Hall . . . Now about Patricia—how would you like to have your sister's old bedroom, my dear?

PATTY. Oh, could I!

CANTRY. It's yours . . . I hope you'll like it here, Patricia.

PATTY. I love it already. The campus is so beautiful—so peaceful—

FRAN. Yes . . . the world keeps its distance . . .

CANTRY. Yes . . . Yes, it does. (*She and* FRAN *smile, en rapport*) Emmy will help you with your bags . . . Good luck, both of you. (*She playfully shoos them out and, with their departure,* CANTRY *looks after the girls, and speaks, musingly:*) I'm so happy to have her back! . . . And Patricia—she's rather a sweet child. Of course she is a little impulsive. . . . Still, I'm sure Frances will keep her in hand . . . Frances will be good here. . . .

LAURA. (*Her agreement stems from long habit*) Oh, gracious yes—I entirely agree with you.

CANTRY. (*Amused and irritated*) Of course, my dear—you always do.

LAURA. (*Nettled; uncomfortable*) Oh no, Auntie Sara—it's just that . . . that . . . (*Her voice peters lamely away*)

CANTRY. (*Smiling*) It's all right, Laura—don't chafe . . . (*Narrowly, deliberately*) Just keep your eye on them, will you?

LAURA. (*Meekly*) Yes, Auntie Sara.

THE LIGHTS DIM QUICKLY TO DARKNESS

ACT I

Scene 2

. *A Bedroom*

It is a cheerful, sunny room in Fairchild Hall. The furniture is pastel-painted; the beds, bureaus and desks are paired for two occupants. There are two doors; one leads to the hallway and stairs; the other, to a vestibule in which there is a clothes closet, and through which one enters the bathroom.

The time immediately follows the last scene. FRAN, *carrying a bag, enters first. She takes a turn about the room, happy to be back in the quarters she once occupied, her spirits high now that she has landed her job.* PATTY *and* EMMY *follow, each carrying a bag; the suitcase* PATTY *carries is label-covered—a complete record of every hotel she has ever stopped in.*

EMMY. I'll put your bag on the bed. (*She looks around and starts toward bathroom*) Now, let's see—where's your clothes closet?

FRAN. It's right through there, Emmy—beside the bathroom.

EMMY. (*She opens the door and laughs amiably*) Well, bless you, so it is—you know the school better'n I do.

FRAN. (*Smiling*) You're new here, aren't you?

EMMY. I only been here a week . . . You got everything you need? If you ain't, you just call out and I'll bring it!

PATTY *and* FRAN. Thank you . . . Thank you, Emmy. (EMMY *goes out. Immediately she has gone,* PATTY's *constraint breaks, and she whoops for joy—but* FRAN's *happiness is inside her, quiet and calm*)

PATTY. Fran, we're in—we're in! And I love your old room! Look —two beds—two bureaus—everything two-sies!

FRAN. Yes. I hope you like your roommate.

PATTY. Fran, I'll have a *roommate!* I've always died of envy when other girls kept saying "my roommate this" and "my roommate that." Now *I* can say it. (*She notices that* FRAN *simply stands there as in a dream*) Hey, where are you?

FRAN. It's funny, . . . All the furniture is different, but there's something in the room—it'll never change . . . I feel as though I went to sleep for a long time—and Rio and Buenos Aires and Montevideo—they were all dreams. Now I'm awake again. (*Then, in high elation*) Patty, we're home—we're home! (PATTY *lets out a squeal of happiness.* FRAN *laughs, then:*) Come on— better start unpacking.

PATTY. Will you help, Teacher?

FRAN. I'll help, Freshman. (FRAN *helps her unpack. The first dress* PATTY *pulls out of her bag begets a groan from her*)

PATTY. Ugh!—here's that *thing* again! I always hope I've forgotten to pack it—and it always turns up! (*Suddenly, good-naturedly,* PATTY *lets loose at the dress a flood of Portuguese cuss words*)

FRAN. Now, no cussing! Not even in Portuguese. Here—give me that dress. (*She takes the dress, rolls it in a ball and dumps it in the waste-paper basket*) We'll run down to Boston and get you a new one!

PATTY. You mean it? Oh, Fran—I love you like a brother! (*Then, soberly*) But I won't get a single stitch unless you do! And no arguments! You need clothes more than I do and with two thousand dollars a year—

FRAN. (*Interrupting*) Say no more—you've convinced me! (FRAN *turns and as she does, glances out the window*) Patty, look— there's Mrs. Rutledge.

PATTY. (*Looking out*) Fran, she *does* walk like a duck!

FRAN. I told you so. But she's wonderful! One course with her and you'll want to be an astronomer. And there's Dr. Pierce. . . .

PATTY. Fran, will I like them?—will they like me?

FRAN. Of course, Dumpling!

PATTY. How about Cantry?—I especially want her to like me. But isn't she a little—unapproachable?

FRAN. (*Quietly; warmly*) Maybe at first. But after a while I hope you'll be good, close friends. I guess I was lucky. I got to know here better than the other kids did. During the holidays I'd be stuck here—miles from home—and Cantry and I would have the whole place to ourselves. We did everything together. She'd take me to church on Easter morning, and once she decked me out from hat to shoes. She made Christmas Christmas and she made herself my family . . . I love Cantry.

PATTY. And now again . . . (*Deciding*) I guess she's people of good heart.

FRAN. That ain't grammar.

PATTY. But it's sense. I always think of people—I call them people of good heart and people of bad heart. (*Pleased with herself*) Pretty okay, huh?

FRAN. Not very okay. Much too neat.

PATTY. Well, I like to know where people are. They're either here or they're way over there.

FRAN. (*Smiling but serious*) How about the ones in the middle?

PATTY. (*With playful bravura*) No middle ground! Me—I'm an extremist!

FRAN. (*Soberly, gently*) It's not too good being an extremist,

Patty. You get yourself in trouble sometimes . . . You almost got us in trouble today.

PATTY. (*Instantly concerned*) I did? How?

FRAN. Don't frown—wrinkles.

PATTY. What did I do? Tell me.

FRAN. When Miss Cantry and I were talking about Roosevelt's death, you blurted out that you wept like a baby.

PATTY. Well, I did. We both did, didn't we?

FRAN. Yes . . .

PATTY. Well, that's all I said. And it was the truth

FRAN. Patty, I *want* you to be truthful—you know that. But I also want you to be careful. The truth is—well—it's got to be used with caution.

PATTY. You mean I should have lied when she asked us—?

FRAN. (*Interrupting. Hiding her irritation*) Of course not. I just want you to get the other fellow's point of view before you rush in with awkward feet! You see, if you'd bothered to find out how *Cantry* felt about Roosevelt—

PATTY. But Fran, that sounds like double talk. She asked us how *we* felt. I told her. What else could I have said?

FRAN. Forget it, Patty. I guess I can't make you catch on.

PATTY. Well, don't give up—I want to know. What was it *you* said? I remember—something about Harding. (*She thinks about this an instant*) That was a little cagey, wasn't it?

FRAN. Not cagey—tactful! For heaven's sake, Patty, you're the daughter of a diplomat—I shouldn't have to diagram these things for you!

PATTY. (*After a moment. A bit hurt*) Fran, please don't be mad at me. Next time—before I say a word—I'll think ten times.

FRAN. (*With an affectionate smile*) Just once is enough, Baby. (*She slaps her on the rear*) Come on—get to work. (*A knock on the door and* LEE BARON *stands there.* LEE, *a sensitive girl, is no older than* PATTY, *but more quiet, more grave*)

LEE. Hello. They told me I was to room here. . . .

PATTY. (*Cordially*) Well, hello—come on in! . . . This is my sister—Frances Morritt. (*Goodhumoredly*) And you'd better mind your manners because she's a member of the faculty. My name's Patty.

LEE. I'm Lee Barron.

PATTY. We're roommates! (*Then, turning to* FRAN, *proud that she can at last say it*) Fran, this is my roommate.

FRAN. Hello, Lee.

PATTY. (*To* LEE—*with quick friendliness*) What do we do now? Start scrapping about beds?

LEE. Oh, no—you were here first—you have first choice.

PATTY. But I haven't any choice.

FRAN. (*Stepping in good-naturedly*) Here, stop this shilly-shallying. This one's Patty's and that one's Lee's (*Then: lest she gave* PATTY *the better bed*) Or vice versa. (*They all laugh.* FRAN *gathers up toothbrush, toothpaste, etc.*) I'll put this stuff in the medicine chest. (*She goes into bathroom*)

PATTY. I've never been away to school before. Have you?

LEE. Yes—prep school.

PATTY. Oh, fine—then you'll know all the answers. I hope you won't mind if I'm an ignoramus. (*The door bursts open and a girl pokes her head in:* SELMA KEENEY, *a petulant girl with horn-rimmed spectacles. She speaks with loud excitement*)

SELMA. Hey! Any members of the Vidge here?

PATTY. Any members of the what?

SELMA. The Vidge! Oh—new girls! I guess no Vidge members around, huh? Have a nice summer?

PATTY. (*Newsily*) Oh, fine. We got here in August and went to—(*But* SELMA *has already closed the door and disappeared.* PATTY *is amazed at* SELMA'S *sudden loss of interest*) What happened?

LEE. It's just a routine. When they ask you whether you had a nice summer you're supposed to say "super" or "dreamboat"—and leave it at that.

PATTY. But what if you had a stinky summer?

LEE. (*Faintly wry*) Everybody's supposed to have had a wonderful one.

PATTY. I get it. (*Trying it out on* LEE) Have a nice summer?

LEE. (*Soberly*) Dreamboat.

PATTY. You don't sound very convincing.

LEE. (*Evasively*) It was all right, I guess. I was up at Parryville for a few weeks. That's in New Hampshire.

PATTY. What's it like?

LEE. Oh, just a little vacation town. Cottages around a big lake and mountains around the cottages.

PATTY. But it *does* sound dreamboat.

LEE. (*Trying to change the subject*) Oh—it was fine . . . Let me help you with those things, may I? (*She carries some of* PATTY'S *clothes to the closet*)

PATTY. Thanks. When you unpack, I'll help you. By the way, where's your stuff?

LEE. The baggage car was taken off at Worcester. I probably won't get my trunk for days.

PATTY. Gee, that's too bad. What'll you do for clothes until your things arrive? (*Expansively*) Say, you can borrow mine. Anything you want.

LEE. Thank you—I'll manage—

PATTY. But that's what we're supposed to *do*, isn't it?—swap clothes and books and boy-friends? (*She stops the quick spate of words*) Fran says I jabber too much. When I do, you conk me, hear? (*They both smile, intuitively making a pact of friendship*) I hope we'll be friends.

LEE. I'm sure we will. (PATTY *takes a clock from her suitcase*)

PATTY. I hope you don't mind a clock in the bedroom. It's awfully quiet and well-mannered. (*Suddenly the alarm goes off, loud and imperious. The girls burst into laughter.* FRAN *re-enters*)

FRAN. Are you two going to spend the day giggling at each other? (*There is a timid knock on the door*)

PATTY. Come in. (NANCY GEAR *comes in. She is a small, thin girl, nervous and full of anxieties*)

NANCY. I'm in the room next door. I heard you laughing in here and . . . Could I just come in and sit down?

PATTY. (*Gaily*) Sure—come on in!

LEE. Hello. I'm Lee Barron. (NANCY *doesn't speak for an indecisive moment*)

FRAN. I'm Miss Morritt. This is my sister Patty.

NANCY. My name is Nancy Gear. (*She sits on the bed, her manner vacantly detached*)

PATTY. (*Trying the catch-phrase*) Hi, Nancy—have a nice summer?

NANCY. (*Low*) No . . .

PATTY. (*Laughing amiably*) A new girl! She doesn't know the password. You're supposed to say "dream-boat."

NANCY. I—was sick during the summer.

PATTY. (*With quick sympathy*) Oh, I'm sorry.

LEE. (*Trying to put* NANCY *at ease*) Would you like to help us?

NANCY. Could I just watch, please?

LEE. Of course. (*There is a loud commotion—someone running up stairs and calling "Dru! Dru!"* MILDRED CHEAVER *bursts into the room. She is an athletic girl of spare physical strength*)

MIL. Dru! (*Her hope of finding* DRU *here is dampened. A shade belligerently*) Hello! What are you all doing in Dru's room?

PATTY. Miss Cantry assigned us here.

MIL. Is Dru moving? Oh lordy, maybe she's moving in with me! Wonderful! . . . Freshmen, huh? Say, any members of the Vidge been here?

PATTY. We don't even know what the Vidge is.

MIL. The V.V.'s—the Valley Vigilantes. Didn't anybody tell you about Hell Week?

PATTY. What's that?

MIL. The first week of school is Hell Week. You freshmen have to do what the seniors tell you. Fetch and carry. Make our beds. Go to the supply store for cokes. Stuff like that.

PATTY. And if we don't?

MIL. Then you're in Hell. You get hauled up before the Vigilantes. You say nobody's been around to explain it to you?

LEE. There was a girl with horn-rimmed glasses—

MIL. Oh, that's Selma Keeney. She's got a gripe she wants to bring before the Vidge. (*The door swings open, screaming on its hinges, and* DRUCILLA ELDRIDGE *struts into the room. She is proud and hard-driven. Resourceful. Intelligent. She espies* MIL *and there is a Demonstration! They throw their arms about each other, shrieking with delight*)

MIL. Dru!

DRU. Mil! When'd you get here?

MIL. Just this minute! God, look at that terrific sunburn!

DRU. Pretty good, huh?

MIL. Listen! These two girls have got your room.

DRU. They're welcome to it! I want to move up on the third with the rest of the gang! Would you like a roommate?

MIL. Would I!—man, that gives me a charge! . . . Say, I've been looking all over for you. Guess what! The kleps have started!

DRU. Already? What's been stolen?

MIL. Selma Keeney brought a gold fountain pen to school. It's disappeared. So she wants you to call a meeting of the Vidge right away.

DRU. (*Disgustedly*) She fractures me! We've got more important stuff with Hell Week coming up. Did you explain it to the kids?

MIL. Just to these.

DRU. (*Turning to the others. With authority*) What are your names, please? Hall and room number.

PATTY. (*Happy to do the honors*) This is—

DRU. Speak for yourself.

PATTY. (*Taken aback*) My name's Patty Morritt.

DRU. And you?

LEE. Lee Barron. Fairchild Hall—room nine.

DRU. All right—next. (*She is looking at* FRAN, *who is at the closet, her back turned*) Hey, stupid—hall and room number! (FRAN *realizes she is being spoken to. She turns, amused*)

FRAN. Me? Frances Morritt. Fairchild Hall. The office.

DRU. (*Off-balance only an instant. Then, haughtily:*) Oh . . . You're a teacher—taking Miss Van Zandt's place.

FRAN. That's right.

DRU. I didn't know you're a teacher. I didn't know faculty was allowed in girls' rooms.

FRAN. (*A moment. Then, graciously*) Oh, yes—I had forgotten that rule. And it's a good one, too. It protects the girls if their should happen to be a snooper on the faculty. (*With a friendly smile*) But I give you my word—I won't do any snooping.

DRU. (*Also smiling*) Still, it's better to follow the rules, don't you think?

FRAN. Yes, of course . . . (FRAN *starts for the door.* MIL *throws* DRU *an admiring glance. The latter smiles*)

PATTY. Wait, Fran! (*To* DRU) You mean my sister can't come to my room?

FRAN. Any teacher can visit you if she's invited. Isn't that so, Dru? (DRU *is silent and* PATTY *speaks quickly:*)

PATTY. Well, you're invited!

FRAN. Thanks, Patty—but I have to unpack, anyway. I'll see you at dinner. (*She goes out*)

DRU. Now—about Hell Week . . . The Vidge will expect you to wear a white arm-band with your name, hall and room number on it. That's so we can get acquainted. You'll also be required to keep the rec room clean and stand up when a senior enters and—(*She is interrupted by a loud honking of an auto horn, followed by a girl's voice shouting "Dru!"* DRU *goes to the window and calls out:*)

DRU. Bella! Bella St. John! (*As she says the name,* LEE *tenses . . .* BELLA'S *voice is heard calling:* "Hey, Dru—look!")

DRU. Bella, your station wagon's a beauty! I'll be right down!

MIL. What's Bella St. John doing here? I thought she was going to Bryn Mawr this year.

DRU. She is. She just stopped over to show off her new Town and Country. You know what?—she's driving all the way down to Philadelphia! From Parryville!

PATTY. Parryville? That's where you were this summer, isn't it, Lee? (LEE *is silent and* DRU *forges in*)

DRU. You were? Well, come on down and say hello to Bella!

LEE. I—don't know her.

DRU. You don't? I thought everybody knew everybody else in Parryville.

LEE. (*Nervously*) I only visited there—just for a week-end. I never met her. (PATTY *looks at her quickly and* LEE *starts toward the closet on the pretext of putting away her overnight bag*)

DRU. Oh, I see. (*To* MIL) Mil, be an angel, will you? See that all the freshmen hear about the Vidge. And get somebody to unpack my bags, huh? Thanks! (*Certain that this will be done for her, she departs without further ado*)

PATTY. Boy, she sure takes over, doesn't she?

MIL. (*Rearing*) What do you mean—takes over?

PATTY. (*With a lame little laugh*) Nothing. It was just her manner—

MIL. She had something to say—she said it and left. What's wrong with that?

PATTY. (*Nonplussed by* MIL's *vehemence*) I didn't say there was anything wrong. She may be all right—(*She goes to bureau*)

MIL. (*Following her*) She is—she's wonderful! (*Suddenly realizing her outbreak was uncalled for*) What I mean is . . . don't say anything about people until you really know them.

PATTY. (*Over her shoulder to* MIL, *who is dogging her footsteps*) Of course not. Sorry. (LEE *enters inconspicuously, tensely*)

MIL. (*To* NANCY) Look, you're not doing anything. You want to unhelp me unpack Dru's bags?

NANCY. I'd rather stay here.

MIL. Somebody's got to help on Dru's bags.

PATTY. Why?

MIL. (*Turning quickly*) Because she's head of the Vidge! Listen, Morritt—don't start by making yourself unpopular around here. (*To* NANCY) Coming?

NANCY. All right. (NANCY *goes out with* MIL)

PATTY. (*To* LEE) Of all the colossal—of all the nerve! (*But* LEE *is abstracted and makes no comment*) What's the matter?

LEE. What? Oh—yes—I was thinking the same thing.

PATTY. (*Quietly*) Lee, if there's something bothering you—I mean, you told me you spent a few weeks in Parryville and you told Dru—

LEE. (*Tightly*) I didn't tell you I spent a few weeks there. You misunderstood me.

PATTY. Gosh, there I go again—putting my two cents where they don't belong. Sorry. (PATTY *looks at her pleasantly, hoping* LEE *will take up the amiable note. But* LEE *moves away silently.* PATTY'S *smile fades. She carries an armful of laundry into the bathroom.* LEE'S *eyes follow her covertly. She stands there, debating. Aimlessly, she walks to the window.* PATTY *returns whistling, making a show of having forgotten the conversation*)

LEE. Patty? (PATTY *quits whistling*) I *was* lying. I did spend a few weeks in Parryville. I do know Bella St. John.

PATTY. (*Apologetically*) Lee, it's really none of my business. Don't talk about it if you don't want to.

LEE. (*With a little outbreak*) But I've got to—it's on my mind—! (*She controls herself*) I was afraid to see Bella St. John.

PATTY. Afraid? Why?

LEE. Because she knows me. She knows I'm Jewish.

PATTY. Well! You're Jewish—so what!

LEE. So everything! (*A moment*) You asked me whether I had a good time in Parryville. (*Bitterly*) Sure, I had a dreamboat time! I didn't know anybody could be so miserable!

PATTY. What happened?

LEE. I'll tell you about it some time . . . when I can.

PATTY. Lee—doesn't anybody here know about it?

LEE. No . . . Right after I left Parryville, I came down here to be interviewed by Miss Cantry. I had heard what a wonderful school it was—and no prejudice here. . . . But I was still all mixed up by what happened this summer—I was suspicious of everybody—(*Then, more calmly*) Miss Cantry gave me an application and I filled it out. But there was one question—religious

affiliation—I left it blank . . . I handed the application to Cantry. I sat there shaking while she read it. If she asks me what I
am, what'll I tell her? First I decided I'd tell her the truth—then
I decided to lie. The truth—a lie—back and forth! At last I made
up my mind—Jewish!—no matter what happens—even if I don't
get in! (*She pauses*) I can still hear what she said to me. "You're
excellently qualified—and we certainly want you with us." . . .
I got up to go and she stopped me at the door. "By the way—
about your chapel attendance—are you Protestant or Catholic,
my dear?" . . . Something said it for me—it just said itself! . . .
I told her I was Protestant . . . (*After a moment*) At first I was
so pleased with myself! But now I feel worse than ever. . . . I
don't know what to do—

PATTY. Lee—I know it wouldn't be easy, but—why don't you explain to Miss Cantry? She's a swell person—she'll understand.

LEE. But what if she doesn't? What if she sends me home?

PATTY. (*With quick loyalty to* CANTRY) Cantry? She wouldn't!

LEE. (*Hopefully*) You think if I went to her . . . ? (*Then*)
No. . . .

PATTY. Lee, does your family know about this?

LEE. Oh, no. I couldn't tell them—I couldn't hurt them—! (*After
a moment her voice lightens, as if with relief that she has unbur-
dened herself to someone*) It's strange . . . When I lied to Miss
Cantry, I made up my mind not to tell anyone. And now the
first person I meet . . .

PATTY. (*With a quiet smile*) As long as you want to keep this a
secret, I will, too.

LEE. Somehow, I know you will. But that's not what I meant. It's
just that—well, we hardly know each other—

PATTY. Sometimes it doesn't take long for two people to become
friends.

LEE. And we are friends . . . ? Despite what I've told you?

PATTY. Of course we are! And there's no despite about it! Heck! (*In an impulsive movement, she ruffles* LEE's *hair up and laughs.* LEE *relaxes; she smiles*)

THE LIGHTS DIM QUICKLY

ACT I

Scene 3

THE LIGHTS COME UP ON—

The Main Hall

It is a wedge-shaped area between the office on the left and the bedroom on the right. The stairs come down behind the rear wall of the bedroom and we see the landing and a few steps. The Main Hall should be designed to give the illusion of spilling out (upstage) upon a more open area behind the stairway and behind FRAN'S *office. Similarly, downstage, it widens as it approaches the stage apron. . . . The girls use this hallway as the general gathering place in Fairchild. Against a wall, a desk with telephone meant for campus calls. Downstage right, on the wall, a pay phone for outside calls. A small end table, a bulletin board, a few chairs, a handsome carved bench. It is Friday afternoon, a week later. The day is unseasonably warm and the windows are open, admitting a glimpse of students passing on the lovely campus walk.*

Onstage there are a few girls. MARY LOUISE, *a lanky, unprepossessing intellectual is talking in the wall phone.* MATHILDA *is sitting at the table, typing on a portable typewriter. She is completely undisturbed by the portable victrola which is grinding out a popular tune right beside her. To this tune,* SYLVIA *and* SALLY, *downstage right, are jitterbugging spiritlessly. They are both eating ice cream sticks. From time to time, girls enter and leave the scene, dressed either for the week-end, for hockey, or wearing the freshman paraphernalia of Hell Week—conspicuous white arm-bands with their names on them, and black, flat-heeled oxfords.*

THE YOUNG AND FAIR

MARY LOUISE. (*Into phone—intellectual and ethereal*) Now listen, Albert—take my advice. Study your sociology and relegate sex to a subordinate position. Remember, you're at Harvard. (HELEN *and* GLORIA, *seniors, come down the stairs. They are hurrying enroute for class.* GLORIA *is carrying an open algebra book and is coaching* HELEN *for a quiz.*)

HELEN. (*Suffering*) Now don't tell me—don't tell me! A-square minus two A-B plus B-square. Right?

GLORIA. Nope—wrong. You've got it bass-ackward.

HELEN. Oh, damn it, why do I have to take algebra anyway. When I graduate I'm gonna get married. Algebra won't do me a bit of good when I get married.

GLORIA. Well, what course will?

HELEN. They don't teach it here. (*They go out.* SUE, *a senior, enters carrying a set of rolled up maps under one arm and an unfurled, large, colored map under the other. She goes upstairs. Meanwhile, the music has stopped.* SYLVIA *departs and* SALLY *goes upstage to take the record off*)

MARY LOUISE. (*Outraged, into phone*) Well! you'd better forget about *me* if your ideal is Lana Turner! (*She hangs up and starts outdoors.* MATHILDA *stops typing and turns to* SALLY.)

MATHILDA. Hey, who wrote *Crime and Punishment*? Ray Chandler?

SALLY. No, stupid. James Cain. (MATHILDA *takes the sheet out of the typewriter and she and* SALLY *start outdoors.* DRU ELDRIDGE *and* SELMA KEENEY *come in. There is a clutter in the doorway*)

DRU. Gangway, freshmen! (*The* FRESHMEN *make way for* DRU, *who is carrying a theme paper. Then, trying to shake* SELMA *off her heels, she goes down to the desk.* SELMA *is carrying a record album. She speaks petulantly:*)

28

SELMA. All I know is that you promised, Dru!

DRU. What can the Vidge do? We didn't steal your old fountain pen.

SELMA. You promised you'd find out who did. (*Lamenting*) My dad gave me that pen as a going-away present. It was gold and it cost eighty-five dollars. . . .

DRU. Gad, what a fuss! You're always losing things. You shouldn't be so careless.

SELMA. (*On the point of tears*) All right—I'm careless! How about Abby de Forest? Is she careless? Did she just carelessly lose her boy friend's fraternity pin?

DRU. (*Not unkindly*) Selma, every year somebody loses something. When you lose anything at school, you just take your loss and curse the kleps.

SELMA. I'll curse 'em, all right! (*She starts to go*)

DRU. Wait, let me ask you something . . . Hell Week is over to-day, so the Vidge will have to disband. A lot of girls think that's a shame. How about you? Would you vote to continue it?

SELMA. Continue what? Hell Week?

DRU. Oh no. Just the Vidge. After all, we've done a good job—why should we have to quit? If we went on we could—well—keep a watch on things. Maybe we could put a stop to all this stealing.

SELMA. (*Indecisively*) Well . . . The freshmen would be against it. They think you've given them an awful going-over.

DRU. Not any worse than last year. (*With quiet persuasion*) Point is—how can the Vidge find your pen if we're not in existence?

SELMA. (*Weakening*) Understand, Dru,—*I'm* not against it. But the kids'll vote it down.

DRU. (*Realizing she has won her over*) You leave that to me. . . .

If we should have a meeting about it, you be here, huh?

SELMA. I didn't hear anything about a meeting.

DRU. We're not broadcasting it. (BOOTS, *an attractive senior, enters with* MIL. *The latter carries a few typed slips of paper*)

MIL. I've typed up the notices for the meeting. There's one for Weatherby Hall and—(*Seeing* SELMA, *she stops talking*)

DRU. It's all right, Mil. I just told Selma about the meeting. (SELMA *takes her record album upstage to the victrola. In a moment we hear the opening strains of a Bach chorale*) Oh, Boots, will you put this paper in Miss Morritt's box?

BOOTS. (*Taking the sheets*) What is it?

DRU. (*With distaste*) My Autobiography for English I.

MIL. Why stew over it now? You've got until tomorrow to hand it in.

DRU. You know very well I'm going to Princeton for the weekend.

MIL. Did you get your train fare from home?

DRU. One hundred bucks—in this morning's mail. Daddy must have liked my last letter. (*The music, up to now hardly audible, swells.* SELMA *listens concentratedly*)

DRU. Selma, do we have to have that racket? Now be sweet and play it on your own vic.

SELMA. (*Hurt*) It's for Music Appreciation. I've got to learn to appreciate it—it's Bach.

DRU. Well, take Bach to your bedroom, huh? (*The girls giggle and* SELMA *goes back, snaps the record off and leaves*)

BOOTS. (*Referring to* DRU's *paper*) Say, this is about your father.

DRU. Well, I can't tell who *I* am unless I tell who my parents are, can I?

BOOTS. But it's all about him. (*Reading aloud*) "I am the only daughter of H. S. Eldridge. I was born in Eldridge, Pennsylvania, a steel town named after my father. It was his company, The National Steel Corporation, which built the town." (*She stops*) Hey, I thought your father retired.

DRU. (*Abruptly*) Who told you that?

BOOTS. I don't know—I just heard it. (*Reflexively she glances at* MIL, *then away*)

DRU. (*To* MIL, *quickly*) Did you?

MIL. (*Defensively*) Yes. I didn't know there was any secret about it. You told me he retired because of a nervous breakd—

DRU. I did not! I said he went away for a rest—that's all! Now he's right back where he always was.

MIL. Well, that's all I told Boots.

DRU. (*A moment*) All right. Forget it. (*She looks at her watch*) It's almost time for the meeting. Boots, get the girls together, will you?—We'll post the notices.

BOOTS. Dru—About the Vidge. I'm still not sure—

DRU. Oh, Boots—quit it. We run things this year, the freshman do it next year. It all comes out even. . . . Now go on, Bootsie. (BOOTS *goes out*)

MIL. So you're really going to Princeton after all?

DRU. Let's not start that again, Mil. You're still invited if you want to go.

MIL. Why do *you* want to go?

DRU. Why shouldn't I? I like to dance and have fun. Why don't you come, Mil?—I'll pay all your expenses. Why not?

MIL. Because I don't have a good time, that's why! I never have a good time at places like that.

DRU. Why don't you?

MIL. (*Flustered*) Things are always different then. *You* get so different. You suddenly get coy.

DRU. I do not! And if I do—well, you've got to behave differently with boys, that's all! (*Handing* MIL *one of the notices*) Here, post this!

MIL. (*Vexatiously*) I wish you wouldn't order me around!

DRU. I'll do it myself. (*She starts toward the bulletin board*)

MIL. Go on—rush into it! Has it occurred to you that if we can't put the Vidge over, we'll look like a couple of jackasses?

DRU. (*Irritably*) Oh damn it, Mil! (*But she is deterred; she doesn't post the notice . . . At this moment two freshmen,* SALLY *and* GEORGETTA, *enter from outdoors.* PATTY *and* LEE *are with them*)

PATTY. (*Prattling cheerily to* LEE) I thought the earth was a perfect round ball, but Mr. Clayburn says its squashed down as though somebody's been sitting on it. (*Seeing* NANCY *come down the steps*) Hello, Nancy—how do you feel?

NANCY. Much better, thanks.

DRU. (*To* NANCY) Well, Nancy—making up your own rules? No name-band on your arm—no black shoes—

NANCY. I—I've been in the infirmary.

DRU. You're not in the infirmary now.

NANCY. (*Apprehensively*) I've got my name-band in my room. I'll get it. (SHE *starts toward stairs*)

MIL. Don't bother. (*She extends her foot and* NANCY, *in motion, stumbles over it.* MIL *laughs loudly, to* NANCY's *humiliation.* PATTY *rises tensely.*)

DRU. Sorry, Nancy—but I'm afraid we'll have to have you up.

PATTY. Wait a minute! Doesn't your Vigilante Committee take illness into consideration?

DRU. This is none of your business, Morritt!

PATTY. Oh, yes, it is! For the past week you've been flexing your muscles at all of us! But Hell Week's over—so relax! (GEORGETTA *giggles and* DRU *stiffens.* SALLY *pulls her armband off. She throws it at* DRU)

SALLY. Here you are, Dru—catch! (SALLY *and* GEORGETTA *laugh and* MIL *races down toward them angrily. They rush off. Humiliated,* DRU *is motionless for a split second. Then, in angry resolve, she takes one step toward the bulletin board and—with a single movement—posts the notice. She beckons to* MIL *and the latter follows her out of the room.*)

PATTY. Somebody ought to do something about that Dru Eldridge.

LEE. Do what?

PATTY. Search me. But next year—let's not have Hell Week any more! Let's call it quits—abolish it! (FRAN *has entered. She hears the last line. Amused at* PATTY's *rebellious order, she says quietly:*)

FRAN. What are we abolishing?

PATTY. Hello, Fran. The Vidge. I think it's a rotten set-up!

FRAN. (*Trying to hide her annoyance*) I wouldn't get too steamed up over it, Patty. Today's the last day—

PATTY. But there's next year.

FRAN. Next year you'll be a senior—and maybe then you won't think it's such a "rotten set-up."

PATTY. Holy mackerel, when I'm a senior *I* won't want to heckle the kids!

FRAN. Good. Then it *will* be better next year.

PATTY. But as long as we have it there's bound to be somebody who'll act like Dru.

FRAN. Patty, take it easy—don't get so wrought up.

PATTY. I can't help it. I don't like the whole idea of the Vidge. Do you? Do you think it's fair?

FRAN. Well, it's certainly not as big an issue as you're making of it. (*The annoyance is clear now*) Anyway, I want you to keep out of it. I won't have you upsetting things and making trouble.

PATTY. But Fran—listen—Nancy came—

FRAN. (*Interrupting*) I'm not talking to you as your sister! I'm talking to you as a member of the faculty!

PATTY. (*Hurt and still*) Yes, Miss Morritt. (*In absolute silence,* FRAN *goes out. The silence holds*)

NANCY. I'm sorry I got you into anything. . . .

PATTY. It wasn't your fault . . . (NANCY *moves up toward the bulletin board. After a moment:*)

NANCY. Do I have to be at this meeting?

LEE. What meeting?

NANCY. (*Reading*) "A student body meeting to determine whether the Vigilante Committee is to continue will be held Friday afternoon in the Main Hall, Fairchild, at four-thirty. Dru Eldridge."

PATTY. What!

LEE. (*Who has hastened to the bulletin board*) That's what it says. They didn't give anybody much time to see it, did they?

PATTY. And look at that paper! The size of a postage stamp! (*She looks in the direction* FRAN *has gone*) Well? Now what?

LEE. Now nothing. You heard what your sister said. Don't get yourself in trouble—

PATTY. But it's so awful—

LEE. Of course it is, but—

PATTY. (*Caught between what she feels she must do—and her sister's instructions*) But—but—but! Oh, the hell with it! (*She makes a bee-line for the door*)

LEE. (*Putting a restraining hand on* PATTY's *arm*) Patty—what are you going to do?

PATTY. If there's a meeting, we're going to be here—as many of us as I can get together! I'm going to Cantry House and Weatherby—

LEE. It's almost four-thirty now.

PATTY. (*Going to telephone*) Then I'll phone them!

LEE. (*Starting for door*) I'll spread it around Fairchild!

PATTY. Wait, Lee! There's no sense in your getting into a jam!

LEE. Don't be greedy—you can't have all the jam! (*She hurries out*)

PATTY. (*Into telephone*) Hello—give me Weatherby Hall, please. (*At this juncture,* BOOTS *enters, followed by three seniors,* GLORIA, PAULINE *and* CAROL) Look here, Boots, I think it was a dirty deal calling this meeting without giving anybody any notice!

BOOTS. Put down that phone! It's against rules to call between halls until after dinner time!

PATTY. (*Into phone*) What? But I've got to talk to somebody down there! . . . Oh darn it! (*She hangs up and starts down toward pay phone.* SELMA *enters. From now until the meeting starts, the girls—all of them seniors—start coming into the room and their hum of conversation continues until the meeting begins)*

GLORIA. Is this meeting going to take long? I've got a dinner date in Boston.

BOOTS. No. Dru promised it would be a short meeting.

PATTY. (*Bitingly*) Oh, very short! If you blink once, you'll miss it!

PAULINE. None of your shenanigans, Morritt. Don't stall things—we've all got places to go! (LEE *comes back into the room.* PATTY *walks over to her*)

LEE. I gave my job to Amy Butler. She's going to try to get the freshmen together. (DRU *and* MIL *enter with a phalanx of girls,* SUE, HELEN *and* MARY LOUISE. DRU *raises her voice over the din:*)

DRU. All right, kids. It's four-thirty. Let's get started. (*Noticing* PATTY *for the first time*) Well, Morritt! You still here?

PATTY. Yes. I read the bulletin board.

DRU. (*With a laugh*) That's like reading other people's mail! (DRU's *cohorts find this funny*) All right, everybody. Let's get quiet. We all have things to do—and I want to catch the 5:20 to Boston . . . We called this meeting to decide whether the Vidge is to go on. I don't think a lot of talk is necessary. We either want it or we don't want it. (*She glances at* BOOTS, *who has been coached*)

BOOTS. I move the Vidge continue!

MIL. I second that!

PATTY. Wait a minute! I see no sense in railroading it through—especially when there are so many girls who are against it!

DRU. That's what we're here to find out!

PATTY. I just want to ask one question. Why do we have to have it? The Vidge has had its traditional week—why continue it?

DRU. There's a very good reason why we have to continue.

LEE. What reason, Dru?

DRU. There's a kleptomaniac in the school. And the Vidge intends to get to the bottom of it!

LEE. How?

DRU. Lots of ways! We could set a trap for the thief!

PATTY. Oh, talk sense! Suppose you did set a trap. Do you think the klep wouldn't find out about it? And if we caught her, what would we do with her? Put her on trial?

DRU. Why not?

PATTY. What kind of trial? Like this meeting?

DRU. What's the matter, Morritt—was Hell Week too tough for you? Couldn't you take it?

PATTY. Of course I could take it—but why should I? Why should the other kids? And why do you want to put us through it? Boots —Mary Louise—Sue—what fun do you get out of it? (*An instant's pause*) I don't like the Vigilantes—and I don't think any of you do, really!

DRU. Speak for yourself, Morritt.

PATTY. (*Blazing*) I am speaking for myself! (*She sees* FRAN *enter. Silence.* PATTY *is tongue-tied for a moment, realizing she is doing precisely what* FRAN *forbade her to do. Whether to go on or not? She goes on, defiant of everybody, even her sister*) I hate the whole idea of the Vigilantes! I hate its name—and I hate being bullied! Now I've said it—(*Confronting* FRAN)—and I don't care who hears me!

FRAN. (*Quietly*) Patty, it serves no purpose to get hysterical.

PATTY. I'm not hysterical—I'm mad!

FRAN. Until you're calm, it might be better to keep out of this.

PATTY. If I keep out of it, Dru gets her own way! Is that what you want? Are you on her side?

DRU. That's a laugh! She's your sister! If she's on anybody's side—

FRAN. (*Interrupting angrily*) I'm on nobody's side! (*Then, checking herself*) I didn't want to get mixed up in your meeting. But I have a personnel job—and this can become serious. . . . Now I refuse to discuss the Vigilante Committee itself. Whether it's right or wrong—I won't be drawn into that.

PATTY. (*Quiet now*) Then what did you come in here for?

FRAN. I'm interested in this meeting's procedure, that' all! If you decide you want the Vidge—all right!—but decide it fairly! . . . Can you understand that?—Dru?—Patty?

PATTY. I'm afraid I can't. I don't see any fair way to do an unfair thing . . . Why don't you ask Dru why there are so few girls present? Or isn't that a question of—of procedure?

FRAN. I think it's a fair question . . . Well, Dru?

DRU. We've got notices posted everywhere. If the girls don't want to come, I can't drag them here, can I?

FRAN. I just saw one of those notices. It was just like this one— very small—and quite hidden. Dru, why didn't you call this meeting openly? (*Quickly—to the others*) Listen—all of you. Keep the Vidge or kill it, as you like. But remember—this affects more than just a dozen girls—it concerns the whole school. You may have your Vigilantes—if you can square it with everybody— if you can square it with yourselves. Now I ask you—each of you —to decide on your own. Don't be bullied—and don't be afraid. Of me—or anybody else. (*Pause. She goes out. An instant's silence*)

DRU. (*Exploding*) Talk about being bullied—she's trying to bully us!

MARY LOUISE. Let's vote!

DRU. All right. Those in favor of continuing the Vidge—signify! (*She raises her hand.* MIL *is the only one to follow her example. Some of the girls laugh . . .* DRU *lowering her hand—ominously*) I said all those in favor! (*No other hands are raised.* MIL *slowly lowers her hand*)

GLORIA. Look here, Dru—there's no sense making a stink about this. All those opposed! I'm voting *no!*

HELEN. (*Raising her hand*) Me, too. I don't care about the damn Vidge!

PAULINE, HELEN, and MARY LOUISE. Count me in . . . I'm against it, too. . . . Let's skip the whole thing . . . (*All hands are raised now, except* DRU'S *and* MIL'S)

GLORIA. Come on! Let's break it up! (*It is the signal for a hurried and confused exit of the girls.* PATTY, LEE *and* NANCY *go out together, in silence.*)

DRU. (*As the girls walk out, all around her*) Scared! Scared of a teacher! The hell with you! (*She storms up the stairs. Now only* BOOTS, SELMA *and* MIL *are left onstage. The latter lashes out:*)

MIL. Well, you two certainly turned yellow, didn't you?

SELMA. After all, Miss Morritt—she *is* a teacher.

BOOTS. And she was talking sense!

MIL. You didn't think so before the meeting!

BOOTS. She didn't talk before the meeting!

MIL. Dru and I . . .! I was the only one who stuck by Dru . . . the only one! I hate girls! (*She starts to go out quickly*)

SELMA. (*With a simper*) You don't like boys, either.

MIL. (*She strides back to* SELMA *menacingly*) Take that back!

BOOTS. Oh, don't get in a lather. It's all over. (*Suddenly, from upstairs,* DRU'S *voice, excited and imperative:*)

DRU'S VOICE. Mil! Boots! Mil!

MIL. (*Calling up*) What's the matter? What is it?

DRU. (*Streaking down into the room*) Did you take the money out of the envelope on my bureau?

MIL. No . . . I didn't!

DRU. It's gone!

SELMA. Gone? How much?

DRU. A hundred dollars!

MIL. Did you look everywhere?

DRU. I know exactly where I left it. Right with my father's letter. Here's the letter . . . here's the envelope . . . but no money!

BOOTS. It was a check, wasn't it?

DRU. No. Cash. I cashed the check at lunch time.

SELMA. Don't worry . . . maybe it'll turn up.

DRU. (*Biting*) Sure! Like your fountain pen turned up . . . or Abby's pin! (*Sweeping all three girls with the force of her words*) There . . . you see! That's what I wanted the Vidge to go on for! To prevent things like this!

BOOTS. Are you making all this up, Dru?

DRU. I knew you'd say that!

BOOTS. Well, *are* you?

DRU. (*Desperately*) No . . . I swear I'm not! I swear by anything you want me to name that I lost that hundred dollars!

BOOTS. God! . . . Well, there goes your trip.

DRU. I don't care about the money—I can wire for more. But who stole it—who stole it?

SELMA. That's one thing we'll never find out.

DRU. Oh, yes, we will! I'll find out!

BOOTS. How?

DRU. You may think the Vidge is dead—but it's not! I'm going on with it! And anybody who's my friend is going on with me!

MIL. Dru—don't do anything foolish!

DRU. (*Her anger bringing her to tears*) Is it foolish for me to want my money back? Is it foolish to want to punish a thief? . . . Are you with me or aren't you? (*Nobody answers. Her hurt flares*) I see you're not my friends!

MIL. Of course we are, but—

DRU. (*Interrupting*) Sure! You were all my friends when you wanted something, weren't you? When you want a date, Selma, you're my friend, aren't you? And when you wanted an angora cardigan on your last birthday, I bought you one, didn't I, Boots—because you were my friend! And Mil is my *best* friend! (*Weeping with fury*) But when my money is stolen—and all I want to do is get it back—I don't have any friends, do I? Do I?

MIL. (*Quietly—unwillingly*) Yes, you do. I'm with you.

BOOTS. But if we go on with this, we're bucking everybody. The faculty—the girls—everybody!

DRU. There's nothing wrong in trying to catch a thief, is there? All I'm asking is—will you help me? Boots?

BOOTS. (*Insecurely*) All right.

DRU. How about you, Selma? Do you want your pen back? Or do you want to sit around and wait until your last nickel is stolen?

SELMA. Well, if the others . . . All right. . . . But if anybody hears about it . . . I don't want to get in trouble . . .

BOOTS. (*Tightly*) How do we go about it? I don't even have a suspicion of who the thief might be.

DRU. But I do!

MIL. You do?

DRU. Yes! A damn good suspicion! (*She turns on her heel and leaves them . . . Suddenly, it is as if a pall of dread had descended upon them. Pause.*)

BOOTS. (*Namelessly apprehensive*) It's going to be awful around here. . . .

SELMA. I wish I hadn't given in to her.

BOOTS. Once you do give in there's no stopping.

MIL. (*The dread has caught even her*) No . . . there's no stopping. (*They look at one another—not directly—but with furtive, frightened glances.*)

THE LIGHTS ON THE MAIN HALL DIM QUICKLY, TO A BLACKOUT

END OF ACT I

ACT II

Scene 1

The Center area of the stage is in half light that permits us to see a few girls coming and going through the main hall. From the school grounds we hear girls calling to one another, the sounds of a volley ball game, the tinny tinkle of a bicycle bell. In the darkness, from Left Stage, the low, amiable laughter of girls in conversation. As the lights fade Center Stage, they come up full, Left Stage, on—

The Office

It is early the following afternoon—Saturday. FRAN *is behind the desk, meeting with three students. They are* GLORIA, PAULINE *and* MARY LOUISE, *the lanky intellectual. There is a pleasant, relaxed air about the group.* FRAN *is studying the social calendar, counting up the number of events.*

FRAN. . . . seven, eight, nine. That makes nine social events for the coming year. Plenty of work for the Social Committee. So you'd better hop to it.

PAULINE. Miss Morritt, before we break up, there's one thing. If the Drama Club is going to put on *Cyrano de Bergerac,* I think we ought to have men playing men's parts.

MARY LOUISE. Please don't bring that up again. You know we can't get any men.

PAULINE. Why not? Look at all the men's colleges in Massachusetts. According to statistics, there are three men for every two girls. That's one-and-a-half apiece.

GLORIA. Yes! Why, in Harvard alone—

43

MARY LOUISE. If we have to get our men from Harvard, things have come to a pretty pass.

PAULINE. You're just against having men in the play because you want the part of Cyrano.

MARY LOUISE. That's not true! (MISS CANTRY *enters, carrying a stack of record cards. She stands behind the girls and her presence is noted only by* FRAN. CANTRY *listens interestedly*)

FRAN. Wait a minute. Mary Louise, what's the feeling of the rest of the Drama Club?

MARY LOUISE. (*With vast superiority*) Well, you know these silly girls. With them the play is *not* the thing!

FRAN. (*Restraining a smile*) I see. If you decided to have men, your job as president of the Drama Club would be even more difficult than it is. Who'd have to get the men?—you. Who'd have to telephone them for rehearsals?—coach them privately—?

MARY LOUISE.—*Me?* (FRAN *nods*) Understand, I'm not against a little extra work. And I do admit they'd add a note of realism. (*Then, unable to restrain her eagerness*) All right—I yield the point.

FRAN. Good. I guess that's about all, girls. Thanks for coming in. (*The girls go out, agog and happy. They notice and greet* MISS CANTRY. *When they have gone:*)

CANTRY. (*With warm congratulation*) Frances, you're very good with them! How I wish every teacher could remember what it was like to be a schoolgirl!

FRAN. Thank you, Miss Cantry.

CANTRY. (*Indicating the record cards*) I've been going through these personnel cards. You don't mean to tell me you've interviewed all these girls in this one week?

FRAN. There's still half the school to go through.

CANTRY. But this is excellent. And your judgments are very wise, Frances! . . . Except in one or two instances.

FRAN. Then I wish you'd straighten me out on them.

CANTRY. Well, Nancy Gear, for example. Do you really think she should not have been admitted to the school?

FRAN. I don't know. I don't think Nancy's well. She spent all last week in the infirmary with a severe headache. Dr. Barrett doesn't seem to find anything physically wrong with her. But he does believe something's ailing the girl.

CANTRY. (*With gossipy intimacy*) Frances, Dr. Barrett is an excellent physician—but he's a terrible alarmist.

FRAN. He thinks she ought to be out of here and under the care of a psychiatrist.

CANTRY. (*With a scoffing laugh*) Oh, he's such an old woman! Psychiatrist, indeed! (*A knock on the door and* EMMY *enters, carrying a glass of iced tea*)

CANTRY. Oh, thank you, Emmy. (*Looking at tray, the rebuke clear behind her sweetness*) You've forgotten the lime again, you know.

EMMY. (*Nervously*) Sorry, Miss Cantry, but chef—he says he's out of limes.

CANTRY. Well, lemon, then . . . All right, you can take it away. (*With an irritable movement she waves* EMMY *out of the room*) So Barrett thinks we should send Nancy home, does he? Now, you wouldn't want to do that to the poor child, would you?

FRAN. Naturally, I don't want to hurt Nancy. But if we keep her here—

CANTRY. (*Interrupting, with a smile*) How about Mildred Cheaver? What do we send *her* home for?

FRAN. (*Uncomfortably*) I—I have a feeling Mil would be better off in a co-educational school. Yet, it might be the worst possible thing for her. Point is, I don't know—I'm not a psychiatrist. . . . There are two or three others who I feel shouldn't be here—

CANTRY. But they are here, my dear. And we can't afford to send them home—any of them.

FRAN. The semester is only a week old. I feel sure we can get applicants to fill their places.

CANTRY. (*Gently*) Frances, you don't understand. It's not a question of getting girls to fill their places.

FRAN. Then I *don't* understand.

CANTRY. My dear, if all our girls had I.Q.'s above one hundred, if they were all without ache or anxiety, we wouldn't have a personnel job here—and you wouldn't be in it. But unfortunately we sometimes have to admit students who are on the borderline. . . . You see, I knew about the Gear girl. Her mother told me she was inclined to—well—melancholy.

FRAN. Yet you took her . . .?

CANTRY. (*Troubled*) Frances, we're working toward an endowed school—I told you that. Well, the Gears are wealthy people—and we never know from what quarter gifts may come. But we do know that gifts don't come for nothing. We have to work for them—perform special services. . . .

FRAN. What kind of special services?

CANTRY. Well, we've got to see what we can do for Nancy. After all, we don't *know* there's anything wrong with the child. We might do her considerable good here. And if we do, it's a feather in our cap. Her mother will be grateful.

FRAN. But suppose—in some way—we make a botch of Nancy?

CANTRY. (*With warm affection*) With you in this office, there'll be no botch—I'm sure of it!

FRAN. I'm grateful for your confidence—but do we dare risk it?

CANTRY. Believe me, the risk is small—and the reward can be so great! (*As* FRAN *looks at her in surprise,* CANTRY *goes on, urgently*) Oh, yes! We have to think of such things, Frances. Forty years ago monetary rewards would have meant nothing. But I owned the school then. It was a small cottage with a blackboard in the dining-room, but I owned it! Down to the last piece of chalk, it was mine. . . . Until the depression, when I nearly lost everything. So I borrowed money—a great deal of it. And with that money came the trustees. And they've been with me ever since. When the trustees beckon, I come. When something goes wrong, I apologize. If a popular teacher should marry and depart, Cantry's losing her grip! If it rains on Commencement Day—if there's an accident on the hockey field—Cantry was negligent! . . . The school isn't mine, Frances. And I can be dispossessed by the shift of a figure in a ledger. One day they'll say "Cantry's too old." Then I *will* be dispossessed . . . unless I can wipe out those debts. And only an endowment will do it. (*She faces* FRAN) If Nancy Gear stands between me and the loss of my school, shall I push Nancy Gear aside?

FRAN. (*After a moment, quietly*) I hope you get your endowment.

CANTRY. You're new at the job and you're earnest—so it's natural for you to worry. But, my dear—try not to worry too much.

FRAN. If Nancy is to stay on, I think we'll need some help.

CANTRY. Help? What kind of help?

FRAN. Well, I thought—a visiting psychiatrist. . . .

CANTRY. You're not joking, are you?

FRAN. Not at all. It would be so much safer! (*She goes to desk and picks up a slip of paper*) Dr. Barrett gave me the name of a good man. Here it is—Dr. Frank Masters. I could telephone him and—

CANTRY. (*Interrupting*) Now, Frances—think a moment, my dear. It's out of the question.

FRAN. Why?

CANTRY. Suppose Mrs. Gear were to hear that Nancy is under a psychiatrist's care? That's precisely what she doesn't want.

FRAN. Good heavens, that's the most stupid, false pride—

CANTRY. Whether it's false pride or not, she wants Nancy treated as a normal child in a normal atmosphere. And suppose the other parents were to hear that we have a psychiatrist around —! Or the trustees—! They'd think we were running some kind of—of asylum here! (*Then, a clear directive:*) Frances, please—don't belabor the point! (*Confused, worried,* FRAN *pauses. At last she puts the slip of paper back on her desk*)

CANTRY. Thank you, Frances. (*She hands her the record cards*) Now, put these cards away and relax. Your worst week is over and you're doing magnificently. (*She goes to the door and notes that* FRAN's *sober look still holds*) By the way, you're not worried about the thefts, are you?

FRAN. Shouldn't I be? Oughtn't I to be doing something about them?

CANTRY. There's only one thing we can do—go through the girls' rooms. But it's an open acknowledgment that one of our girls is a thief.

FRAN. Unfortunately it's the truth.

CANTRY. But is it wise to let that get around? The only advantage in a search is that it satisfies the girls we're doing something. The hunt is always fruitless—it just yields a contraband ash-tray or a wine bottle. (*She smiles and* FRAN *joins her, wryly*)

FRAN. I wish I could take it as philosophically as you do.

CANTRY. (*Affectionately*) Don't worry—you will. Heavens, you must, if you're to have any peace of mind. Boarding schools are always having outbreaks like this. There's a run of thefts and then—presto—it stops. (*With a laugh*) It's like colds before Christmas or measles in the spring. Nothing to worry about. . . . Well, have a nice week-end.

FRAN. Thank you. (CANTRY *stops at the door when she sees that* FRAN *is putting on her glasses, intent on continuing work. She returns to* FRAN's *desk*)

CANTRY. Come on now—stop slaving. (*She goes to* FRAN, *leans over to her and gently removes the reading glasses from* FRAN's *face.*) And let's take these frightful things off. (FRAN *smiles at her and rises. In a flood of genuine warmth,* CANTRY *continues.*) Frances, you'll never know how happy I am you're back. I missed you when you were graduated—and thought of you so often! You're the only one who has ever made me regret that I never married, that I never had a daughter. (*They hold upon one another in a moment of deep affection.* CANTRY *takes a few steps toward the door and remembers* FRAN's *glasses. With a little laugh.*) Oh—here. (FRAN *comes to her and takes her glasses.* CANTRY *goes to the door. A parting word, with mock bossiness:*) Now do as I say, child—relax! (*She is gone.* FRAN's *pleasant mood fades when her eyes alight on the slip of paper that carries the psychiatrist's name. She takes up the paper and her sense of disturbance, plaguing and intangible, again assails her. She looks at the door, thinks of* CANTRY—*crumples the paper and tosses it in the wastebasket. . . . There is a knock on the door.*)

FRAN. Come in. (PATTY *opens the door narrowly and enters. She has not seen* FRAN *since their altercation yesterday—and her manner is strained. So is* FRAN's)

PATTY. Hello, Fran. If you're busy . . .?

FRAN. I'm not busy, Patty.

PATTY. (*Waiting an instant*) I—wanted to apologize about yesterday. I'm sorry I was such a brat.

FRAN. (*Gently*) Were you a brat?

PATTY. (*With quick contrition*) Please don't be kind to me. I was so damn self-righteous about the Vidge. Then you showed up at the meeting, and you handled it so—cleverly. . . .

FRAN. (*Disturbed by the word "cleverly"*) Patty, you do understand that I couldn't show any partiality—I couldn't come out flatfootedly against the Vidge? I had to put it on the basis of—well—procedure.

PATTY. (*Doubtfully*) Yes . . .

FRAN. You're disappointed in me.

PATTY. (*Quickly*) Not in you, Fran! I just feel that we won on a technicality instead of a . . . (*She hesitates, loth to use the word*)

FRAN. A principle? (PATTY *nods*) But we did win on a principle, darling—the principle of democratic procedure. Anyway, what difference does it make how we won so long as we did?

PATTY. (*Not quite sure she believes this; yet she wants urgently to recapture her rapport with* FRAN) Of course . . . that's the important thing. (*Anxiously*) You know, Fran, we never used to quarrel. . . . How did it happen? (*Abruptly, with a small outcry*) Oh, Fran, it was awful!

FRAN. I know. . . . It stayed with me.

PATTY. Me, too. I couldn't sleep.

FRAN. No more quarrels, Dumpling.

PATTY. Right. (*Instantly, the apprehensions vanish; they are smiling at one another.*) Jumpin' jehosophat, look at the bags under my eyes! Fran, I'm getting ancient! (FRAN *laughs and* PATTY *joins her.*) Oh, it's as pretty as April outside and Hell Week is over and the Vidge is as dead as a herring and Lee and I are going to see Abbott and Costello!

FRAN. Oh, I wish I could go with you!

PATTY. (*Eagerly*) Can you—will you?

FRAN. No . . . work to do. (*She hands* PATTY *a composition paper*) Here's your autobiography, Patty. You got a B-plus. What an interesting family you have—and what whopping lies you tell about them!

PATTY. Just trying to make it pleasant reading.

FRAN. I was fascinated. You sounded like Mata Hari.

PATTY. (*After a moment, soberly*) Have you graded Lee's paper?

FRAN. Did you know about it?

PATTY. Yes . . . It's been on her mind, Fran. She's been wanting to come and talk to you—but she just couldn't. But now that she's been able to write about it. . . . She's out in the hall now. Will you see her?

FRAN. I don't know what good it'll do, Patty. It's something she'll have to work out for herself.

PATTY. I know. But she needs help. Please see her, Fran. (FRAN *nods and* PATTY *goes to the door and calls*) Lee! (LEE *enters and stands at the door, tense and tentative.* FRAN *smiles with quiet friendliness*)

FRAN. Hello, Lee. Come in. (*Pause*) I've read your paper, Lee. You write very well. . . . Lee, this will be very difficult for both of us. . . .

LEE. I know, Miss Morritt—so you needn't soften anything—
I've been preparing myself. . . .

FRAN. There must be so much more than your paper tells. . . .
Will you answer a question?

LEE. Yes.

FRAN. Are you—please don't mind my asking this—are you
ashamed of. . . .?

LEE. Of being Jewish? No, I'm not. If I were, it would mean I'd
be ashamed of my mother and father. And that's not so—I love
them—they're good people—I'm proud of them! (*Then, wryly*)
They could have reason to be ashamed of me—not I of them.

FRAN. Well, what *do* you feel about it?

LEE. (*Confused. With difficulty*) I—don't know. I just go along
like anybody else. I guess I don't feel any different until something happens. . . .

FRAN. Like what?

LEE. Like somebody accusing my father of being aggressive.
Like being told by one of the girls at prep school that I mustn't
sing Christmas carols. . . . Then I know I'm separate—and I
feel separate! I've been feeling that way more and more—and
this summer it frightened me—

FRAN. What happened this summer?

LEE. It sounds so trivial. . . .

FRAN. Go on.

LEE. I—this summer four of my friends got the idea of going up
to Parryville for a month. It was an awfully gay idea—just the
five of us—no family—no chaperones. We'd get a little cottage on
the lake—rent a canoe. . . . We didn't think our parents would
let us—but they did. (*She pauses and* FRAN *helps her*)

FRAN. Were any of the girls Jewish?

LEE. No. I was the only one. But Connie Philips—she has dark hair and an olive complexion—she looks more Jewish than I do. (*Again she pauses*) Well, we went up there. We found the loveliest little house right on the lake. We went to see the real estate agent. He took one look at Connie and he said, "The owner's given me instructions—I can't help it—I can only rent to certain people." There was no mistaking it. Connie told him she wasn't Jewish and for a moment it looked like the cottage was ours. But I couldn't help it—I got so furious I said, "Connie's not—but I am!" (*She moves away from the desk*) We couldn't rent a thing. At last we wound up in a ratty little bungalow where the furniture wasn't clean and. . . . At first the girls were on my side. But the place was so awful! They couldn't help resenting me, I guess. . . . Two weeks later Bella St. John came up with her family. On the Fourth of July, Bella gave a party. . . . Only four of us were invited.

FRAN. Did the others go?

LEE. No. I begged them to, but they wouldn't. . . . That night —we could hear the music from Bella's party across the lake. It was a dreadful evening. The five of us stayed in and played bridge. Then somebody said, "Even for bridge there's one too many!" It started like that—just a joke. . . . But it didn't stop there. They started quarreling—with me and among themselves. Connie—my best friend—I guess she was getting hysterical. I know she didn't mean it but she said. "You had to open your Jew mouth!". . . . I went home that night. . . . My family was vacationing in California— I was alone in the house. . . . (*Tensing more and more*) I didn't tell anybody—I kept it inside me. It worked on me and worked on me. . . . I'd pick up a book and if the word was on a page it would be the first word I'd see. (*Trembling*) I wanted to get away some place where I'd never hear the word again—where nobody would know me—where I wouldn't get hurt again! . . . So I came here—and I lied to Miss Cantry.

PATTY. (*Gently*) And the pity of it is—if you only knew Miss Cantry!—it wouldn't have made any difference if you had told her the truth!

LEE. Miss Morritt, would I have gotten in if I had?

PATTY. Why shouldn't you be permitted here? Why, Fran? Why should she have to lie to be like everybody else?

LEE. Well, I did lie. And now I feel I've done something dirty. Have I, Miss Morritt, have I?

FRAN. (*Gently*) I don't think you've done anything dirty, Lee.

LEE. Then how do I get rid of this feeling? Shall I tell Miss Cantry about myself? Shall I keep quiet? What?

FRAN. Lee, I don't know. All I know is what I myself feel. I think you're a fine person—nothing else matters to me. And I believe most people in the school feel the same way. So I see no reason for you to make an issue of this. And if you choose to keep your silence—I can see nothing wrong in it.

PATTY. But, Fran—something *is* wrong with it—I don't know what—but something! If she keeps quiet she'll be giving in to rotten people like that real estate agent in Parryville—

LEE. I don't think he was to blame.

PATTY. Somebody's to blame! The people who owned the cottage, maybe. They're forcing her to lie and hide and run away! And why should she do that? (*Then, forthrightly*) I think she ought to go to Miss Cantry and tell her everything!

LEE. Miss Morritt, that's what I want to do.

FRAN. (*With reservation*) If that's what you want to do, then do it—by all means, Lee.

THE YOUNG AND FAIR

LEE. But you think it's not a good idea?

FRAN. Lee, you lied to Miss Cantry—but it wasn't the worst lie in the world, and heaven knows you were provoked to it! Why go on punishing yourself—why look for new heartaches—why stir up a hornet's nest?

LEE. Hornet's nest . . . ? (*Quietly*) Then it's true—I *wouldn't* have gotten in if I had told the truth.

FRAN. (*Quickly*) I didn't say that.

LEE. Miss Morritt—I've got to know—is there any antisemitism here?

FRAN. (*Defensively*) I've never seen any. (*Quickly*) Lee, let me put it this way: If I were interviewing you for admission to the school—I'd accept you and be happy you had chosen to come here.

LEE. And Miss Cantry—?

FRAN. I'm sure I can make the same answer for Miss Cantry.

PATTY. Then if Cantry feels that way, why shouldn't Lee go to her—?

FRAN. (*Exasperated*) Because if there's an issue, nobody will win. Nobody ever has. It's an ancient sore. Let it alone.

LEE. (*Quietly*) I've tried that, Miss Morritt. It won't heal. (*She starts to go, but* PATTY *puts a restraining hand on her arm*)

PATTY. (*Quietly, pleading*) Fran, I don't want to quarrel with you again, but—look—Lee needs some help. I don't know—maybe if you went to see Miss Cantry with her—

FRAN. You're very brave with somebody else's skin. What you're advising might ruin Lee's life at school!

PATTY. What you're advising might ruin her life!

FRAN. I'm advising nothing! I'm simply trying to—(*She stops herself. More evenly*) Patty, in my job I've got to keep things on an even keel. I've got to *quiet* disturbances—I daren't *cause* them! I've got to consider the school and Lee and everybody else—and do what's best!

PATTY. (*Impulsively*) You mean what's safest!

FRAN. (*Stung, she loses her temper*) Patty, I think you'd better leave this room! (PATTY *is so startled she doesn't move. But* FRAN *has turned on her heel, not daring to face* PATTY *for fear of making matters worse. Quietly,* PATTY *slips out of the room. Unaware that* PATTY *has gone,* FRAN *remains quite still. Then, without turning, she says softly:*)

FRAN. I'm sorry, Pat. . . . (*When she gets no answer she turns and sees that only* LEE *is left in the room with her. The quiet lasts. . . .*)

LEE. Miss Morritt, forgive me for. . . .

FRAN. (*Worriedly*) Never mind that. What are you going to do?

LEE. I don't know. . . . Miss Morritt, I don't ask you to go to Miss Cantry with me. Just tell me and I'll go by myself.

FRAN. Why in heaven's name did you bring me this problem! Why did you create it in the first place!

LEE. (*Quietly*) I didn't create it, Miss Morritt. It was there when I was born. (*She starts for the door*)

FRAN. (*Contrite*) I shouldn't have said that. I was thinking of Patty—I—

LEE. It's all right. . . . Thank you for listening to me. (*She goes out.* FRAN *paces unhappily a few moments until her eye falls on* LEE's *autobiography, which lies forgotten on the desk. She takes it up and hastens to the door to give it to* LEE)

FRAN. Lee! (*But* LEE *is out of earshot.* FRAN *closes the door, tosses the paper on the desk and simply stands there. A knock on the door.* FRAN *is so preoccupied she does not answer. After a moment,* NANCY *enters. She carries a slip of paper*)

NANCY. Miss Morritt, would you sign this for me, please?

FRAN. What is it, Nancy?

NANCY. An excuse note from the nurse. It needs your signature, too. (FRAN *reaches for it, signs and wordlessly returns it.* NANCY *starts to go, then stops at the door*)

NANCY. Miss Morritt, will you tell me something?

FRAN. (*Still preoccupied*) Yes?

NANCY. Dru Eldridge said I was to come up before the Vidge for not wearing my Hell Week clothes and I was wondering—

FRAN. (*Slightly curt*) Forget it, Nancy. The Vidge is over.

NANCY. I don't think it is. I just saw Selma. She says the Vidge is reorganizing secretly.

FRAN. (*Abruptly attentive*) She must have been teasing you.

NANCY. Oh, no—she wasn't. Dru's getting the Vidge together so she can get back the money she lost. And Selma—

FRAN. You say Dru lost some money?

NANCY. Yes. Didn't you know?

FRAN. How much?

NANCY. A hundred dollars.

FRAN. Where was the money?

NANCY. I don't know—Selma didn't say.

FRAN. (*Half question, half statement*) Dru's going to continue the Vidge . . .? (*Suddenly she picks up the phone and speaks into it*) Dru Eldridge, please.

NANCY. (*Alarmed*) Please don't tell them I told you. It's supposed to be a secret.

FRAN. Don't worry, Nancy. (*Into phone*) Hello—Dru? Miss Morritt. Can you come down for a moment, please? (*As she hangs up, she sees* NANCY *looking at her, nervous and distraught*)

NANCY. Miss Morritt—please—I don't want to get mixed up in it.

FRAN. I won't mention your name—there's nothing to be nervous about. (*She studies her. Then, gently:*) Sit down, Nancy. . . . I'm glad to see you out of the infirmary. How do you feel?

NANCY. Much better, thank you. It was just a headache, you know. I get them quite frequently.

FRAN. You have some work to make up—but take your time doing it. Meanwhile, get to know the girls—make some friends. I don't suppose you've been able to do that, stuck away in the infirmary.

NANCY. Lee and Patty came up to see me nearly every day. They've been swell. So far, they're the only ones I feel—uh—easy with.

FRAN. Before long there will be many others. I should like to be one of them. . . . If you ever have anything that's troubling you . . .

NANCY. (*She looks away an instant. Something is worrying her; she isn't quite sure whether to take the opportunity* FRAN *has given her to discuss it. At last:*) Miss Morritt—there *is* something. Does the school—? Will the school let my mother know I spent the first week in the infirmary?

FRAN. I suppose so. Why?

NANCY. Does Mother have to be told?

FRAN. Don't be concerned about it. If she knows you're feeling better now—and that we're looking after you—she won't be worried.

NANCY. No, it's not that. Mother thinks I make it up—about having headaches. She says I get headaches to get out of doing things and meeting people. If she hears I've been in the infirmary she'll be terribly angry.

FRAN. (*Puzzled*) Angry?

NANCY. Yes. Mother thinks I'm a—coward. But I'm not! I can do things that take a lot of courage—!

FRAN. (*She darts a glance at* NANCY. *Then, quite quietly*) What kind of things, Nancy? (*When* NANCY *doesn't answer—in order to make it easier for her:*) Is there anything else that's worrying you?

NANCY. (*Simply*) No. I just wanted to explain about Mother, that's all.

FRAN. (*Gently*) Nancy, as you know, some girl in the school has been behaving foolishly—she's been taking things. (NANCY *nods*) She may be doing it because she's—not well. And if she comes to tell me about it I may be able to help her.

NANCY. Miss Morritt, I was in the infirmary when Abby's fraternity pin was stolen. And I think the same person did all the stealing, don't you?

FRAN. Yes, I rather believe so.

NANCY. If you'd care to search my room—or my belongings—?

FRAN. No. Forget about it.

NANCY. (*With complete simplicity*) I haven't stolen anything, Miss Morritt.

FRAN. (*She looks at her and* NANCY *returns her glance openly.* FRAN *relaxes*) No—I'm sure you haven't. I'm sorry I asked. (*She rises*)

NANCY. (*Also rises*) That's all right. (*There is a knock on the door and* DRU *enters*)

FRAN. Hello, Dru. Sit down.

NANCY. Thank you, Miss Morritt. (*She departs*)

FRAN. (*To* DRU) I'll be with you in a minute. (*She goes to the pile of theme papers on the filing cabinet and looks for* DRU's *paper. Her back is to* DRU *who is sitting close to* FRAN's *desk.* DRU's *eyes rove the room, then fall on* LEE's *paper on the desk. Her attention caught, she reads the paper without touching it. Then, taking a quick glance at* FRAN's *turned back, she takes the paper up. . . .* FRAN *turns. Neither speaks for an instant. Then:*) May I have that, please?

DRU. (*Poised—as she hands it back*) Oh, it's Lee's—I thought it was *my* autobiography.

FRAN. I have yours here, Dru. (*She selects another paper from the stack on top of the filing cabinet and hands it to* DRU *who accepts it wordlessly and waits . . . Trying to be casual*) Dru, you got permission to leave for Princeton. How is it you're still here?

DRU. (*Politely*) Something happened—I was delayed.

FRAN. You lost some money, didn't you?

DRU. Yes. I had to wait for my father to wire me some more.

FRAN. I'm sorry about your money, Dru. We'll do everything we can to find it. (DRU *deliberates for an instant, then decides, audaciously, to anticipate* FRAN's *question about the Vidge. She affects her most ingratiating manner:*)

DRU. Miss Morritt, I think I know why you asked me down here. You've heard about the Vigilantes. Isn't that so?

FRAN. (*Momentarily disarmed*) Yes . . .

DRU. I'm glad, because I wanted to talk to you about it. (*Then with studied sincerity*) Miss Morritt, at first we thought we'd continue the Vidge in secret. But—honestly—we don't want to do anything underhanded. So if you'll give us your permission—

FRAN. (DRU'S *manner is suspect. However,* FRAN *speaks as forthrightly as she hopes* DRU *is*) Dru, you know I can't give my permission after the girls voted against the Vidge.

DRU. (*With elaborate sincerity*) Miss Morritt, all we want to do is put a stop to the stealing. Surely you can't object if we volunteer to give our time to it.

FRAN. Dru, please don't try to maneuver me into agreeing that the Vidge is a splendid thing—

DRU. Well, what's wrong with it? You want to find the stolen property—so do we! You want to find the thief—so do we!

FRAN. (*Interrupting*) Dru—how would you do these things?

DRU. I don't know yet. But if you'll just trust us—we'll find some way.

FRAN. (*Narrowly*) *Why* do you want to do all this? Surely, it'll be a lot of bother—and not at all pleasant. Why?

DRU. (*Disarmingly*) Well, I admit I've got a personal interest. After all, a hundred dollars . . .

FRAN. I know it's a considerable sum—but does the money mean that much to you? Is that the real reason?

DRU. I don't know what you mean.

FRAN. (*Annoyed*) What *is* the reason? (*When* DRU *merely stares at her:*) Doesn't it have something to do with a pleasure you get out of being in command?

DRU. (*Injured*) Is there anything wrong with that?

FRAN. (*Restraining her anger*) That depends. If you seize the command against everybody else's will—if you use the command to frighten and terrorize people—

DRU. Who says I'll do that!

FRAN. You're practically saying it now. And right there—you've said it openly in your paper!

DRU. (*Flinging the paper on the desk*) Where! Show me where!

FRAN. Oh, it's not in any particular line—but it's all through! Your malice shoots out in so many directions. At things you know nothing about. Labor unions, for example—

DRU. Unions! I know more about them than you do.

FRAN. (*Controlling herself*) Dru, I didn't mean to discuss unions. I know very little about them.

DRU. But I do know! I know from my father! He got a rotten enough deal to know them inside out! And they're all crooked! All of them—they're run by racketeers and criminals! And I hate them all!

FRAN. (*Quietly*) There! That's what I mean . . .

DRU. (*Her fury, her remembered heartbreak, spill out in an inchoate flood*) I've got a right to hate them! My father's fights with unions nearly killed him. During the war, they spread lies about him! They called him a traitor and dragged him up before the Senate! When it was over he was a sick man—in a sanatorium! Do you know what it's like to see your own father—! (*With a quick intake of breath, she reins herself in, angry that she has revealed her heartbreak. But this exposure, showing that* DRU *is not all steel and arrogance, gives* FRAN *hope. She moves toward* DRU's *side of the desk and speaks quietly*)

FRAN. Dru, I'm sorry about all that. But I beg you—don't carry your father's hatreds into your own life!

DRU. (*Tightly*) Listen, Miss Morritt, my father has the right answer. You know what it is? "Buy 'em or beat 'em!"

FRAN. Dru, that answer will get you a lot of grief!

DRU. But it works—I've found it works! Let me tell you something, Miss Morritt: Once I was an ugly little kid—afraid of everything—always scared! When my parents were divorced, I lived alone in a big house—and nobody came near me. I'd be alone at school and I'd be alone at home. You know how I worked it out? I started to go to school with my pockets full of toys and candy—I found that if I wanted a friend, I had to buy one. And pretty soon I knew how to get people to do things for me. When you've found that out, you know all the answers!

FRAN. (*Quietly*) Did the answers work for you yesterday, Dru? You lost the vote, remember.

DRU. (*Bitterly*) I wouldn't have if you hadn't interfered!

FRAN. Did you find that the girls flocked to you after it was over? Did they sympathize? How many girls are on your secret Vigilante Committee? How many real friends do you have in the school?

DRU. (*The questions hit home. Unhappily*) They were *all* my friends until you came!

FRAN. Were they your friends? Or did you buy them with house parties and week-ends at Princeton? . . . Are you still giving out candy and toys, Dru?

DRU. (*Whirling away from her*) What difference does it make?

FRAN. (*Relentlessly*) It does make a difference to you, doesn't it? (*Then, quietly*) Dru—listen. You're losing ground with the girls—and you know it. You'll continue to lose ground until you learn you can't go at people with a rubber hose. And the first step is to give up this strong-arm committee of yours.

DRU. (*With an outcry*) I can't! By now the whole school knows about the Vidge. If I back out, I'll look ridiculous!

FRAN. For a while maybe. But soon we'll have a student government here—a real student government. I want you to help me organize it—I want you to be my friend—

DRU. You're trying to bribe me with your friendship!

FRAN. (*Simply*) Yes I am. It's the best thing I have to offer.

DRU. I've got to go on with the Vidge!

FRAN. Dru, what good will this do you!

DRU. If the Vidge succeeds—if we find the thief—

FRAN. Then you'll probably find an unstable girl who should be in the care of a doctor, not a Vigilante Committee. What if one of your own friends were guilty? Mil, for example—

DRU. Are you insinuating that Mil Cheaver is a thief?

FRAN. I'm merely trying to show you that this is a more delicate thing than inexperienced girls can handle. If it were Mil, you'd say she's not a thief—she's an ailing girl—

DRU. Now you're saying vile things about Mil! I'm not going to listen to any more of this!

FRAN. You see, you really *can't* handle it—you can't even discuss it! (*Then, more quietly*) I promise we'll try to get to the bottom of this. And I ask you to disband your committee! Please.

DRU. I can't—not now—don't you see I can't! I'll be a laughing-stock!

FRAN. Very well, then—you leave me nothing else . . . You're not to leave the grounds until you decide to give it up.

DRU. (*In a fury*) You mean you're campusing me?

FRAN. Yes.

DRU. I've invited six girls to Princeton. I'm going away for the week-end!

64

FRAN. If you do you'll be suspended from classes!

DRU. You can't do that! I'll get my father on the phone! (FRAN *makes no rejoinder*) My father's on the board of trustees, Miss Morritt! (*Just the slightest movement from* FRAN) You didn't know that, did you? (FRAN *remains quite still*) Well? Now may I go to Princeton?

FRAN. You may not. Unless you disband the Vidge.

DRU. (*In a frenzy of rage*) I won't disband it!

FRAN. I hope you change your mind!

DRU. (*Almost hysterical*) I won't change my mind! You said you wanted to be friends! Well, we're not going to be friends! I'm your enemy! And I'm going to get even—you see if I don't! (*She thunders out of the room*)

THE LIGHTS DIM RAPIDLY

ACT II

Scene 2

The right side of the stage is illuminated quickly and we see:

The Bedroom

No one is there. A knock on the hall door, then DRU *streaks into the room, wild-eyed and out of breath. She looks about her disconnectedly, then goes quickly to one of the bureaus and opens a drawer. Abruptly, the hallway door opens and* MIL, *also breathless, stands on the threshold.*

MIL. Dru! For Pete sake, what are you doing?

DRU. I'm going to search every bedroom—until we find the thief. I'll show Miss Morritt the Vidge can do what she can't!

MIL. Dru, you'd better get out of here!

DRU. No! I'm going to show them all that there's a *need* for the Vidge—

MIL. But you'll get in trouble!

DRU. I'll risk it!

MIL. Do you have any idea who the thief is? You said you had a suspicion.

DRU. I had to say that, stupid—to show the girls I knew what I was doing. (*Going toward bureau again*) Come on—let's get started.

MIL. Oh, Dru! I'm sure Lee didn't take anything—and if you suspect Patty, you're off your trolley!

DRU. I don't suspect anybody, I told you! I only hope—I hope Patty did do it!

MIL. Don't talk so crazy! You know darn well she's not the kind to—

DRU. How do we know she *didn't* steal those things? And I tell you—if she did—she and her sister will be out of here so fast—!

MIL. You're doing this out of spite! You're just trying to get back at Miss Morritt!

DRU. Why shouldn't I? She's trying to trim me down to a no-body! It's her against me! She's got to leave this place—or I've got to! And anything I can do to get her out—

MIL. (*Frightened*) I don't want to have anything to do with this! (*She starts for the door*)

DRU. Wait a minute! (*Sincerely affected*) You're—walking out on me . . .?

MIL. (*Unhappily*) Dru, let's call it off—forget about it!

DRU. (*Quietly*) What are we calling off? Our friendship?

MIL. No, of course not! I mean *this*—all this sneaking around and—

DRU. Miss Morritt was right. When it comes to a showdown, I've got nobody. I've got to do it alone!

MIL. (*Desperately*) Dru, don't you understand? All this business —it makes me feel scared and—sick. If you gave a damn about me you wouldn't ask me to—

DRU. I do ask you! (*Then, quietly*) I ask you to prove that Miss Morritt was wrong—that I do have friends—that they'll stick to me!

MIL. Oh, Dru!

DRU. Well?

MIL. (*Quietly, trembling*) No . . . (*With an outcry*) No! It costs too much to be your friend, Dru—it costs too much! (MIL *rushes out of the room.* DRU *stands there, immobilized, in an agony of loss and frustration. What to do? She paces, starts for the door as if to make it up with* MIL—*and give up the whole project. But she can't. At last, quieting the turmoil inside her, she makes her decision:* DRU *goes toward the bureau and resumes her search . . . Suddenly, offstage, the sound of running footsteps.* DRU *shuts the drawer, frightened. She freezes as she hears a knock on the door.*)

NANCY'S VOICE. Lee! (DRU *looks around for an escape; she races toward the closet. At this precise moment,* NANCY *enters and sees the closet door closing.*)

NANCY. Lee! Lee—is that you? (DRU *comes back into the room cautiously. She is about to make an excuse for her presence here when* NANCY, *who is carrying some objects in her hand, makes a panic-stricken movement to hide them behind her back.* DRU *sees this.*)

DRU. (*Measuredly*) Hello, Nancy.

NANCY. (*Tense*) Hello. I heard voices in here. I thought it was Lee.

DRU. What do you want Lee for?

NANCY. I—just wanted some—some advice. But it's nothing—I'll come back. (*She makes a jerky movement toward the door.* DRU *steps quickly into her path.*)

DRU. Wait a minute . . . There's no rush, is there?

NANCY. (*Stopping tensely*) I'm in a hurry—I—

DRU. What for? What are you so nervous about?

NANCY. I'm not nervous. Please let me go by.

DRU. (*Quickly*) What have you got behind your back?

NANCY. (*Retreating*) Nothing.

DRU. Let me see it, huh? You'd better give it to me, hadn't you?

NANCY. (*Breaking away in panic*) It's not yours!

DRU. (*Suddenly making a grab for* NANCY) Give it to me!

NANCY. (*Struggling—crying out*) Please—let me alone! (*She tries to break away but* DRU, *stronger, subdues her. The struggle is over—and* DRU *has the objects in her hand.*)

DRU. (*With a gasp*) My God! The pen and the fraternity pin and my money—everything! (*As* NANCY *collapses on the bed*) So *you've* been doing the stealing . . .

NANCY. (*In a frenzied confusion*) I don't know—I don't know— (*She begins to sob*)

DRU. You'd better come along.

NANCY. (*Resisting*) Where? Where are you taking me?

DRU. Miss Cantry. (*She tries to shepherd* NANCY *toward the door*)

NANCY. No—please—she'll send me home!

DRU. I'm sorry, Nancy. But the Vidge set out to find the thief. Well, we've found her.

NANCY. Please—! I won't take anything again—I promise! My mother—I don't know what she'll do to me! Please help me out!

DRU. Look, I can't go protecting a girl who—

NANCY. I'll do anything you say—anything!

DRU. I'm sorry it's you, Nancy—but it had to be somebody. (*Suddenly, struck by inspiration, she drops* NANCY'S *arm*) Wait a minute . . . Why does it have to be you?

NANCY. You will help me, won't you?

DRU. Be quiet—let me think! (*Suppressing her excitement*) **What did you come into this room for?**

NANCY. Miss Morritt asked me if I'd taken the things. And I said no—

DRU. (*Quickly*) Did she believe you?

NANCY. I think so. But then I got scared. I didn't know **what to do.** I thought Lee would tell me what to do.

DRU. (*Quietly—with studied friendliness*) Nancy, you know you're in a tough spot. Not only could you be sent home—you could be arrested.

NANCY. Please help me—

DRU. If I do, it's liable to get me in trouble.

NANCY. No—no, it won't!

DRU. If I protect you, you've got to back me up. Because I'd be taking a big chance for your sake.

NANCY. (*Snatching at the straw*) Of course—I understand—I'll back you up.

DRU. And you'll have to stay in with me until the very end. It would be bad for both of us if something went wrong. (*With elaborate solicitude*) And it would be still worse for you, Nancy.

NANCY. I know—I'll do whatever you say.

DRU. All right . . . Here—take this stuff. (*As* NANCY *obeys,* DRU *quickly moves to* PATTY's *bureau. She opens the second drawer, searches around, then comes up with a stationery box.*) Put the things in this stationery box.

NANCY. But it's Patty's!

DRU. Never mind that—do as I tell you! (*As* NANCY *complies*) Now put the box in this bottom drawer.

NANCY. It's Patty's bureau—I couldn't do that!

DRU. (*Impatiently*) All right—if you don't want me to help you—! (NANCY *puts the box in the drawer*) Shut the drawer. (*As* NANCY *shuts the drawer, we see* PATTY *and* LEE *enter the Main Hall downstairs.* LEE *starts up the stairs.*)

PATTY. (*Calling*) Hurry up, Lee. We'll miss the main feature.

LEE. I'll only be a minute.

NANCY. (*Frightened*) Lee's coming up the stairs!

DRU. Oh, dammit! (*Quickly improvising*) Go round the bend in the hallway. When Lee comes in here, stand outside the door. Listen to everything that goes on in here. (NANCY *goes.* DRU *quickly surveys the room. Downstairs* PATTY *has picked up a book and is reading. Upstairs,* LEE *breezes into the room. On seeing* DRU, *she halts. As if in slow motion, she puts down the books she is carrying*)

LEE. What are you doing in our room?

DRU. I'm making a search of all the rooms in Fairchild.

LEE. Did you get Miss Morritt's permission to do that? Or Miss Cantry's?

DRU. I have the permission of the Vidge. That's enough.

LEE. The Vidge doesn't exist. And you can't search in here. (DRU *smiles*) Oh, for goodness' sake, do you think we stole your money?

DRU. I don't think anything. But I'm going to fine-tooth-comb this school. Every single room.

LEE. I won't allow you to touch a thing in here.

DRU. Then you make the search while I watch.

LEE. You won't get me to search anything!

DRU. If you're innocent, why do you object to it? (*A moment*) Now don't waste time or I'll make it pretty tough for you. (*Quietly*) And believe me, I can!

LEE. (*Apprehensively—in a strained voice*) It's useless anyway—none of the stolen property is here!

DRU. (*Casually*) All right—let's see. Why don't you start with that bureau—?

LEE. I can't go rummaging in Patty's things—

DRU. (*With studied impatience*) Oh, don't be silly. You're *clearing* her by doing it.

LEE. (*Opening the top drawer of* PATTY'S *bureau*) There! There's nothing in any of these drawers. You can see for yourself. Scarves —sweaters—three blouses—nothing else.

DRU. (*Offhandedly*) Okay—try the next one.

LEE. (*Opening the second drawer*) It's all her art stuff. Brushes, paints— (*Suddenly she comes upon the stationery box. She opens it and, seeing its contents, gasps. Quickly collecting herself, she closes the drawer. In a tight voice:*) Nothing there.

DRU. (*Quickly*) What was in that box?

LEE. Nothing, I tell you—nothing! (*But* DRU *has now opened the drawer herself. She pulls out the box. Opens it.*)

DRU. Holy—!

LEE. (*Quaking*) She—but—where did they come from?

DRU. They came from Abby and Selma and me!

LEE. Patty can't—she doesn't know anything about those things!

DRU. Maybe they just sneaked in by themselves!

LEE. Or maybe they were sneaked in by somebody else! By you, perhaps! (*Abruptly moving toward the door*) I'm going to ask Patty whether she knows anything—

DRU. Wait, Lee! (*Suddenly her tactics change. Almost sympathetically*) I had no intention of searching the rest of the school. I knew the search would stop here.

LEE. (*Infuriated*) Of course you did!

DRU. (*Building, block by block*) I knew it would stop here because I was tipped off about Patty.

LEE. (*Savagely*) Tipped off! By whom—Mil Cheaver?

DRU. (*Measuring each word*) No—by somebody else. Somebody in this school saw Patty with that fountain pen this morning!

LEE. You're a liar!

DRU. The girl came into this room without knocking. Patty was standing in front of this bureau—with the pen in her hand. When Patty saw the girl she quickly opened that drawer. And then she was furious at the girl for barging in!

LEE. I don't believe it!

DRU. If I ask the girl who saw her with the pen to come in here, will you believe *her?*

LEE. No, I won't!

DRU. Maybe you will when you see who the girl is. (DRU *goes swiftly to the door, looks down the hall and beckons to* NANCY. *Without an instant's pause:*) I know how you feel about this, Lee—and I don't blame you. But somebody did steal that stuff—

LEE. Not Patty—

DRU. Listen, you can never be sure of anybody! Who can tell what's eating Patty? Maybe there's something wrong with her —something we don't know about—

73

LEE. Don't say that! (NANCY *is now at the door,* LEE's *back is to* NANCY, *but* DRU *sees her.*)

DRU. (*Indicating* NANCY) All right, Lee—look! (LEE *turns and sees* NANCY)

LEE. (*Shaken*) Nancy!

DRU. (*Gently, to* NANCY) Nancy, tell Lee what you told me. Didn't you see Patty with that pen this morning?

NANCY. (*Her eyes down—faltering*) Yes.

DRU. Where was she standing?

NANCY. It was—I—in front of the bureau—

LEE. (*Going to pieces*) Nancy, you must be wrong! Are you sure it was this fountain pen? Don't make a mistake, Nancy!

DRU. (*As* NANCY *hesitates*) No—don't make a mistake.

NANCY. Yes . . . it was that one. I'm sure of it.

LEE. Nancy—listen—

DRU. Don't, Lee. Can't you see how this is getting her all upset? She didn't want to have to tell, did you, Nancy? (NANCY *shakes her head. She is unstrung*) Go on back to your room, Nancy. (NANCY *leaves*)

LEE. (*Breaking out*) I can't believe it! Something must be wrong—!

DRU. Of course! Something *is* wrong—with Patty. Otherwise, I couldn't believe it myself . . . Now, what are we going to do about it?

LEE. (*Crying out*) I'm not going to do anything!

DRU. But we've got to! You and I have got to take that box to Miss Cantry!

LEE. Me?—I won't!

DRU. I'm not asking you to lie or anything. I just want you to—

LEE. You're asking me to call Patty a thief!

DRU. You needn't call her anything! Just tell Miss Cantry that you and I discovered the stolen property in Patty's stationery box.

LEE. (*Desperately*) I won't!

DRU. What if you're asked? Will you lie?

LEE. If I have to—yes!

DRU. Lee, don't be a fool! Why make yourself her accomplice? (*In a movement of flight,* LEE *starts for the door.* DRU *stops her. Ominously:*) If you lie, you know what'll happen, don't you?

LEE. You can't do anything to me.

DRU. Oh yes I can! I'll show them what a liar you really are! You lied to get into the school! You know you people aren't allowed at Brook Valley! I'll expose you—as a liar!

LEE. (*Wildly*) What's Patty got to do with that? You can't persecute Patty because of me!

DRU. (*Quietly*) Look here, Lee. The stolen articles were found in this room. This is Patty's room—but it's also *yours!* (*Insinuating*) If Patty didn't steal those things, who did?

LEE. You don't think I did?

DRU. No, but there might be others who'd think so. There are lots of people around here who wouldn't throw you out because you're a Jew—but they'd jump at the chance to throw you out as a thief!

LEE. (*She grips the two ends of the bureau and hangs over it, shaking*) Oh, God!

DRU. Now, remember. All I'm asking is that you tell the truth. That's all—the truth—you discovered the box in Patty's bureau. If Patty's innocent, she'll be able to prove it! (*In the hallway,* PATTY *walks to the stairs and calls:*)

PATTY. Lee, where are you?

DRU. (*Rapidly—in a whisper*) Now listen to me—don't sacrifice yourself!

PATTY. Lee!

DRU. You don't want to see her now, do you?

LEE. (*At wit's end!*) What'll I do—what'll I do—

DRU. Come on. Come into my room. She won't see you. Come on —we'll talk about it some more—come on— (LEE *hardly hears* DRU. *She behaves as though she were sleep-walking.* DRU *gets the stationery box, takes* LEE *gently by the arm, leads her out.*)

THE BEDROOM GOES TO DARKNESS

ACT II

Scene 3

The lights come up quickly on—

The Office

Some minutes after the close of the preceding scene. FRAN *is busy at work.* EMMY *enters with dustpan and brush.*

EMMY. Can I straighten up a bit, Miss Morritt?

FRAN. Yes, come in, Emmy. Will I be in your way?

EMMY. No, ma'am . . . Saturday I like to do a lot of cleanin'.

FRAN. I guess it's a good day for it—with most of the girls away.

EMMY. Yes'm . . . Miss Morritt, are you going to be using Miss Cantry's office regular now? If you are, I'll put your stuff away. (*She indicates a pile of books and writing paraphernalia on top of the filing cabinet*)

FRAN. No, thank you, Emmy. I'll only be in here a day or so. My own office is almost ready.

EMMY. Oh, it's the little corner room, isn't it? With the new green carpet.

FRAN. Yes.

EMMY. I wondered about that. That'll be nice for you. It don't look like an office at all—more like a little parlor.

FRAN. Yes, it's very attractive, isn't it?

EMMY. Mm. Just like everything else around here—real nice and attractive . . . I never worked in surroundin's like this before.

(*With a little laugh*) It kind of rubs off on a woman. (*She giggles infectiously and* FRAN *joins her . . .* CANTRY *and* LAURA *come in abruptly*)

CANTRY. Come back a little later, Emmy. (EMMY *nods, takes up the waste-basket, dustpan and brush and goes toward the door. The freight she is carrying is too much for her and as she tries to close the door after her, the waste-basket falls and makes a loud clatter on the floor.* CANTRY, *startled, turns in annoyance*)

CANTRY. For heaven's sake, Emmy, must you always be clumsy!

EMMY. Sorry, Ma'am. (FRAN *helping her,* EMMY *quickly gathers up the spilled contents of the waste-basket and departs.*)

CANTRY. That woman!—she's been here two weeks and she's worse than ever! I should never have hired her!

FRAN. (*Noting* CANTRY's *unnerved manner*) Is anything wrong?

CANTRY. Frances, I'm afraid so. Laura, tell Miss Morritt.

LAURA. Well, I overheard the most disturbing thing in the art studio—(*Suddenly turning to* CANTRY) Oh, Auntie Sara, the girls are painting an abstract of Emily Dickinson—all birds' wings and flower petals—

CANTRY. Never mind that, Laura—go on.

LAURA. (*To* FRAN) Well, I heard Selma Keeney tell Helen Priest that a lot of money was stolen from Dru Eldridge's room.

FRAN. Yes . . . I just heard about that.

CANTRY. Has anything been done to recover Dru's money?

FRAN. Not yet. As I say, it was only in the last half hour that—

CANTRY. We must do something at once.

FRAN. Forgive me, Miss Cantry, but a short time ago you said there was nothing to worry about—that thefts were like colds before Christmas—

CANTRY. I know. It's a nasty business and I didn't want to think about it. Now I'm afraid we must.

LAURA. (*Fluttering*) Oh, I should say we must! A hundred dollars is a good deal of money.

FRAN. (*Trying to smile pleasantly*) Not nearly as precious to Dru as that fraternity pin was to Abby.

LAURA. But this is Drucilla.

FRAN. You mean if something is stolen from Abby the matter is trivial, but if something's stolen from Dru it's momentous?

LAURA. Well—yes.

CANTRY. Nonsense, Laura. (*To* FRAN) It's just that Abby and Selma are placid children—they don't make difficulties. Dru might . . . As a matter of fact, I'm sure she will. Laura tells me Dru's all wrought up about that meeting of the Vidge yesterday. I do wish you hadn't opposed their silly little committee.

FRAN. Don't you think a little opposition is what Dru needs? That girl's in a bad way—we've got to try to straighten her out.

CANTRY. That's a lifetime job—and you have two semesters.

FRAN. Well, I've already begun on it.

CANTRY. (*With quick apprehension*) You have? How?

FRAN. I've restricted her to the campus until she—

CANTRY. You've campused Dru Eldridge? Good heavens!

FRAN. I had to, Miss Cantry. The girls voted against the Vidge— but Dru took things into her own hands. I had to stop her.

CANTRY. Frances, I've tried to explain to you. Running a school isn't just a matter of reading, writing and arithmetic. There are parents to consider—and trustees!

FRAN. (*Worried*) I know—and Dru's father is one of them.

CANTRY. You mean you knew that—and yet—?

FRAN. She told me after I had already committed myself. If she had told me before, should I have treated her differently?

CANTRY. (*Impatiently*) Frances, Dru's father is one of the few friends I have left on that board! How can you be so casual about that?

FRAN. Miss Cantry, I'm not being casual, but—

CANTRY. (*Breaking out*) Oh, yes, you are—very casual! But I can't be! I know what it is to go to one of those board meetings! They sit around that long table like a court of inquisitors. When I scrape through a meeting I thank God and Mr. Eldridge!

FRAN. (*Moved and concerned for her*) I'm sorry—I didn't mean . . . If there's anything I can do—

CANTRY. (*Calmer*) There's only one thing—and I beg you to do it. (*To* LAURA) Please ask Drucilla to come down here. (LAURA *goes.* CANTRY *faces* FRAN) I want you to tell Drucilla you've thought it over and decided that the punishment was a little severe. Remove the campus restriction.

FRAN. Miss Cantry, you can't ask me to do that.

CANTRY. Give her a lighter sentence. Put her on eight o'clock call or even seven—but let her off the campus.

FRAN. But if I back down now, I'll be backing down as long as I stay here. I'll never get anywhere with the girls.

CANTRY. Sometimes a teacher's position is strengthened when she acknowledges herself in the wrong.

FRAN. But I wasn't wrong! Was Dru's punishment unfair?

CANTRY. Frances, this is trifling! . . . You realize I myself can take Dru off campus.

THE YOUNG AND FAIR

FRAN. It's your school, Miss Cantry.

CANTRY. But I don't want to do it that way. I'll tell you what. I'll make it easy for you. Let me speak to Drucilla. I'll do it tactfully. (*Then, pleading*) Frances, don't let your pride stand in the way here. You won't object if I talk to her, will you? Please. (FRAN *turns away, saying nothing, and* CANTRY *accepts this as* FRAN'S *agreement*) Thank you, my dear. You may go if you want—you needn't see her if it'll be embarrassing for you.

FRAN. If I'm going to eat crow, I'll be here to do it. (*There is a knock on the door*)

CANTRY. Come in. (DRU *enters. She is poised and silent*) Drucilla, I've heard that you lost some money. I'm sure it must have upset you dreadfully, otherwise I could find no excuse for your going on with the Vidge.

DRU. (*Innocently*) It's not only the money, Miss Cantry. It's the whole idea of a thief—here—at Brook Valley. If people were to find out about it—

CANTRY. I know—I know—(*Pause. Then, smoothly*) Drucilla— when I was told you were restricted to the campus, I entirely approved. I want to make it clear that I still approve. However, Miss Morritt herself—in thinking it over—feels that your punishment is too severe. So we have compromised. You will be put on eight o'clock call for two weeks. (DRU *smiles inwardly. But she will not accept her triumph without getting direct satisfaction from* FRAN. *With an air of great friendliness:*)

DRU. Is that satisfactory to Miss Morritt?

FRAN. Yes . . .

DRU. (*Weighing her words. To* CANTRY) I want to thank both of you. I only wish you and Miss Morritt had had your discussion sooner . . . before the damage was done.

CANTRY. Has there been any damage?

DRU. Yes. I was supposed to go to Princeton.

CANTRY. You can still go, Drucilla.

DRU. (*Parading her injury*) But I can't! I've called it off. All the girls I invited—they've gone without me—I felt like such a fool!

CANTRY. Dru, why don't you leave right away—you're all dressed and—

DRU. But I've missed my train connections!

CANTRY. Dru, I'm sorry it happened.

DRU. Oh, I'm not blaming *you*! (*Then, with ingenuous concern*) Miss Cantry, I'm so worried! Things are so different in the school this year. Last year everything was swell. Everybody got along with everybody else. There was real school spirit—

CANTRY. I don't notice any difference at all, Dru.

DRU. But the girls notice it! Half the school is against the other half! And the thefts—one right after another! Something's terribly wrong here!

FRAN. (*She can stand* DRU's *subterfuges no longer. Evenly:*) Dru, stop it! In your opinion, I'm what's wrong—is that it?

CANTRY. Please Frances—! Drucilla, the subject is closed!

DRU. Very well, Miss Cantry. (*Darkly*) Now I'd like to open a new subject.

CANTRY. Please—not now! Just go to your room.

DRU. I wish you'd listen to what I have to say!

CANTRY. (*Angry*) You've said enough! (*Long silence.* DRU *speaks quietly*)

DRU. All right. I don't mind waiting. It'll keep. (CANTRY *gives* DRU *a puzzled and startled glance as the latter departs*)

CANTRY. Oh, that noxious girl! And her threatening manner! What do you suppose she's up to?

FRAN. That's a question for an alienist. (The telephone rings, loud and imperious. FRAN *answers it*) Hello. (*Then, with a trace of alarm*) Yes, put it through. (*To* CANTRY) Eldridge, Pennsylvania is calling.

CANTRY. Eldridge! So that's what she was driving at!—she telephoned her father!

FRAN. (*Into phone*) Yes, this is Brook Valley.

CANTRY. (*Unnerved*) He'll want to know about Dru's money—about the thefts! What'll I tell him?

FRAN. Hello!

CANTRY. (*Tense*) Say I'm not in! I've got to have time! Tell him I'm not in!

FRAN. (*Into phone*) I'm sorry, she's not in . . . I couldn't say . . . Very well. (*She hangs up*) He'll call again.

CANTRY. And *then* what'll I say?

FRAN. We've got to tell him exactly what happened.

CANTRY. Tell him the school is infested with thieves? Tell him we punished his daughter because she tried to get back money that was stolen from her?

FRAN. That's Dru's story—not ours!

CANTRY. Her story is the only one that matters! He dotes on that girl! (*Giving vent to her fright*) Oh, Frances, why did you start all this? If you hadn't campused her she would have made no trouble! Why can't you curb these high-flown principles of yours!

FRAN. (*Ruefully*) Give me time . . . I'm new here.

CANTRY. (*Under her breath—like an oath*) Heaven protect me from new brooms!

FRAN. Miss Cantry, why are you berating *me?* Who is at fault? —Dru or I? If I am, tell me how—what have I done?

CANTRY. You've set a vicious trouble-maker on us, that's what you've done! She'll use those thefts against us—with her father, with everybody! (*Taking a spasmodic breath*) Well, here it is! Always I've had an answer for them—but what do I say this time!

FRAN. Miss Cantry—if you'll try to be reasonable—! Things can't be so desperate that—

CANTRY. Oh, can't they! Everybody on that board has a special ax to grind. But Eldridge keeps them in line. I tell you, if I lose Eldridge, I'll lose the school!

FRAN. Please—we'll work everything out—if we can only stay calm!

CANTRY. It's easy for you to be calm! The school's just a job to you. But it's all I've got! (*She suddenly reins herself in*) Frances, we must do something. When Mr. Eldridge calls again, I've got to tell him we've found the thief! And you've got to help me find her!

FRAN. I'll do whatever you say.

CANTRY. Find her—ferret her out—!

FRAN. Shall I call the police?

CANTRY. Of course not! This is all in your hands, Frances— and on your head! (*Abruptly*) Wait! Just a moment! (*Suddenly she goes very still, thinking intently. FRAN watches her, then abstractedly takes up a large paper clamp. Absently, she snaps the clamp open and shut a few times. The clicking noise irritates CANTRY*) Please—don't do that. (FRAN *puts the clamp on*

the desk. CANTRY's *idea is beginning to crystallize*) If I were to
. . . No . . . But what else *is* there? (*Abruptly she makes her
decision. She goes to the desk and sits. She opens one of the
drawers and extracts her personal checkbook. She starts writing
in it.*)

FRAN. (*Apprehensively*) Miss Cantry, what are you doing?

CANTRY. Please call the switchboard and ask them to get the
girls together—whoever is left on campus.

FRAN. (*She goes to phone and speaks as* CANTRY *writes*) Would
you telephone all the halls and ask the girls to come to the office,
please. (*She hangs up*)

CANTRY. (*Without looking up*) Thank you, Frances . . . I can
handle this alone now. (*This is meant as* FRAN's *dismissal from
the room*)

FRAN. (*Without heeding it*) What are you going to do?

CANTRY. I won't involve you any further, Frances.

FRAN. What is it you're sparing me? Why did you write out
that check?

CANTRY. Never mind.

FRAN. Please tell me.

CANTRY. If you're completely lacking in resourcefulness, I'm
not . . . Frances—at whatever cost—I must protect my place
here.

FRAN. (*Edgily*) Miss Cantry—who gets that check?

CANTRY. (*Pulling herself together*) Emmy Foster.

FRAN. Why?

CANTRY. Don't worry. I won't get her in trouble.

FRAN. (*With sudden realization*) You're going to discharge
her—!

CANTRY. Yes! But not for stealing, understand—I wouldn't do that. Merely for inefficiency—and heaven knows we have grounds enough to do so. That wouldn't prevent my telling the girls I *had* discharged her for stealing. I could say Emmy confessed—

FRAN. (*Revolted*) Miss Cantry, you won't do this—

CANTRY. I've got to do it. I have no alternative. (*She rings the bell for* EMMY)

FRAN. Miss Cantry, you're distraught. I tell you—it's wicked—it's—

CANTRY. I would have discharged her anyway!

FRAN. But to discharge her like this—! You're persecuting an innocent woman!

CANTRY. I'm persecuting nobody. She won't even know we're accusing her of anything.

FRAN. She'll leave here in shame. People who knew her with affection—

CANTRY. Nonsense. She's hardly known here at all. She's been here only two weeks.

FRAN. But she'll leave as a thief. She'll never be able to get a job—

CANTRY. She'll leave with a very good reference. A far better reference than I would have given her otherwise. And I'll make her a present of a whole month's severance pay rather than the regular two weeks. How can she lose by it?

FRAN. Even if *she* doesn't lose, *you will!* Miss Cantry, it'll plague you—

CANTRY. (*In an outburst*) Of course it'll plague me! Then why do I do these things?!

FRAN. (*Quickly*) I know it's not for yourself alone—it's for the school! But is it worth it?

CANTRY. (*Passionately*) The kind of school I've worked for—yes, it's worth it! A school that sends out into the world such women as you are— it's worth any expedient!

FRAN. No matter how ugly—

CANTRY. Expedients are always ugly!

FRAN. But where will you draw the line? If you sacrifice a blameless woman—

CANTRY. I've sacrificed myself for this school. Do I count for less than Emmy? (*There is a knock on the door*)

CANTRY. Come in.

EMMY. (*Entering*) You rang, Miss Cantry?

CANTRY. Yes . . . Emmy, we're making a rearrangement of the servants—and we find we can get along with fewer of them. So we're doing without the services of those we hired most recently.

EMMY. . . . You mean you're lettin' me go?

CANTRY. Yes, but it has nothing to do with you personally. I'll see that you get a very fine reference. And I'm giving you more than the two weeks salary—here is a whole month. (*Extending the check*) Your check, Emmy.

EMMY. (*Anxiously, hesitating*) . . . Thank you, Miss Cantry.

CANTRY. Well, that'll be all, Emmy. (*As* EMMY *goes out she glances in* FRAN'S *direction, but the latter turns away, unable to face her. Pause.* CANTRY *collapses in a chair*)

FRAN. (*Turning*) As easy as that . . . (CANTRY *says nothing*) Miss Cantry, you're not going to tell the girls that Emmy's a thief. (*Silence. Then, pleading*) I beg you—don't do it!

THE YOUNG AND FAIR

CANTRY. I have to, Frances.

FRAN. If you do, I'll tell them you're lying! Every bit of it—I'll tell them!

CANTRY. (*Rising*) Frances, listen to me—and listen selfishly. You want to stay on in this school, don't you? Very well, I want to keep you here. But how can I? If you put me in a painful position—how can I?

FRAN. I'll not be a party to this—I don't care if you fire me!

CANTRY. How about Patricia and her education? If you won't think of yourself, in heaven's name think of your sister!

FRAN. I am thinking of my sister! What do I say to her about this? How do I explain it! (*Crying out*) My God, how can you do it!

CANTRY. And how can you be so self-righteous! Don't you see I've been driven back and back until every move I make is decided for me!

FRAN. But *you*—doing *this!*

CANTRY. Show me how to keep my school without doing it! Show me how to stay alive! (*She is overwrought*) When I founded this school, I was as spotless as you are! I thought high —as high as those poplars I planted—nobody could touch me! But when I started to lose the school, I made a concession here and another there—! I've mortgaged my soul to save my life!

FRAN. Well, I won't mortgage mine!

CANTRY. Just wait—watch and wait! If you live in the marketplace, you'll do as I've done!

FRAN. I won't! I won't let it happen!

CANTRY. (*Quietly*) . . . You're going to tell them?

FRAN. (*Entreating*) What else can I *do?*

CANTRY. (*Quietly*) In the space of an hour, the whole world seems to have altered between you and me. An hour ago I said that if I had a daughter—

FRAN. Don't talk about that now!

CANTRY. I meant it an hour ago. I remembered that while you were in school this was your home. I remembered that you wept when you left the school—and so did I!

FRAN. All right!—you're closer to me than my parents were! But how can you take advantage of that?!

CANTRY. And how can you refuse the advantage? I'd not refuse it to you! Why, Frances? For whom? For a woman you'll never see again—a chance creature—?

FRAN. Can I have her on my conscience?

CANTRY. (*In a great outburst*) Then have me on your conscience! Go on—tell the girls I'm lying—and I'll lose my school. I'll have nothing left—nothing! Have me on your conscience! (*Then, in a paroxysm of weeping*) Oh, Frances—Frances—

FRAN. Please—

CANTRY. You won't tell them, will you? You'll do what I ask, won't you? Please—

FRAN. (*The words tearing out of her*) Yes—yes—let me alone!

CANTRY. (*In a flood of gratitude*) You'll never be sorry—never. (*There is a sound of girls gathering in the hallway. Hearing them,* CANTRY *wipes her eyes and collects herself.* FRAN *stands looking out the window, her back to the room*) I'll call them in now. It'll be over quickly—very quickly. (*She takes a deep breath, then opens the door. With difficulty she musters up her old charm*) Come in, girls. (*Four or five girls, including* SELMA, *enter the room*) Aren't there more of you?

BOOTS. Most of the girls are away for the week-end.

CANTRY. (*Calling*) Come in, Mil—Helen. (DRU *comes in with the others, her hands behind her back. She is carrying the stationery box surreptitiously. Nobody, not even the audience, sees the box.* LEE, *her face haggard, is near* DRU. PATTY *comes into the room alone. She espies* LEE *and starts toward her but* LEE *takes a distant seat, avoiding her*) Sit down, girls. I hope you will all spread the good word—and it is a good word. The school thief has been apprehended. She has confessed and has been discharged. It was one of the servants—one of the newer servants—Emmy Foster. (*There is a stir. Whispers*) Now, we haven't been able to recover the property. But perhaps in the next few days—

DRU. Excuse me, Miss Cantry. Are you sure it was Emmy?

CANTRY. (*An almost imperceptible fluttery movement, then:*) My dear, if her confession isn't assurance enough . . .

DRU. It just seems strange, that's all. Miss Cantry, I tried to tell you before but you wouldn't let me. I know who stole those things. But she's not a servant—she's one of the students. And she's right in this room!

CANTRY. Drucilla, please—let me handle this—

DRU. But I have evidence to prove it! Here! Look in this box! Abby's pin—Selma's fountain pen—my hundred dollars!

CANTRY. (*Rapidly*) I—I don't understand it! There must be some mistake! Why, Miss Morritt and I—we were both in the room when Emmy—

DRU. I don't doubt that Miss Morritt had something to do with Emmy's confession! Do you know whose box this is? (*She whirls and faces the girls*) Perhaps she won't own up! (PATTY *moves forward quickly. Her knees are unsteady; her face, pinched*)

PATTY. It looks like mine.

DRU. It is yours!

PATTY. (*In a small voice*) Where did you get it? I don't understand—?

FRAN. (*To* DRU) Just a minute! Are you accusing Patty—?

DRU. Yes! I accuse Patty Morritt of being a thief!

FRAN. You're a liar!

CANTRY. Patricia, do you know anything about this?

FRAN. Of course she doesn't!

CANTRY. Patricia, I'm talking to you!

PATTY. I never even saw those things! I don't know how they got there!

FRAN. Of course you don't! (*To* DRU) You've gone too far, Dru!

DRU. (*Swaggering into the challenge*) What if I tell you I didn't discover the box! What if I tell you Patty was seen this morning with that fountain pen in her hand!

CANTRY. Patricia, is that true?

PATTY. I never saw it, I tell you!

DRU. So you say! But let's find out! Nancy! Nancy Gear! (NANCY, *frightened, steps forward*) Did you see Patty with that pen?

NANCY. Y-yes.

DRU. (*Throwing questions fast*) When?

NANCY. This morning.

DRU. Where?

NANCY. In her room.

DRU. Where in her room?

NANCY. By the bureau.

DRU. (*Turning to the others, triumphantly*) There! You see! (*As* NANCY *starts to move away,* FRAN *takes her by the shoulders*)

FRAN. Nancy, you're mistaken—aren't you? You didn't see Patty with that pen, did you?

NANCY. (*Hardly audible*) Yes. (*She moves away.* PATTY *stifles a sob*)

FRAN. (*Going to* PATTY *quickly*) It's all right, Patty. We'll get to the bottom of this.

DRU. Of course we will! (*To* PATTY) Do you know who discovered these things in your bureau?

PATTY. (*Crying out*) I don't know and I don't care! You've got plenty of friends who can discover all kinds of lying things!

DRU. (*Crowing*) But it wasn't one of *my* friends—it was one of yours! (*She turns to* LEE, *quickly*) Go on, Lee—tell them!

PATTY. (*Breaking from* FRAN—*thunderstruck*) Lee!

CANTRY. Lee, do you know anything about this? (LEE *is unable to speak for a moment*) Go on!

LEE. (*In agony*) Patty, I know you didn't do it!

CANTRY. Lee, did you find that box?

LEE. Miss Cantry—

CANTRY. Did you?

LEE. Yes—(*To* PATTY—*flagellating herself*) Patty, I know you didn't take those things—

DRU. Well, there it is, Miss Cantry!

FRAN. (*She moves entreatingly to* CANTRY) Miss Cantry, I don't know what's happening—but it's vicious! You and I know that Patty's innocent! Please—tell Dru you don't believe a word! Please—tell her!

CANTRY. (*With tortured indecision*) Oh, Frances—Frances—

FRAN. You don't believe it, do you? (*Precipitously, the telephone bell sounds a long, commanding note.* CANTRY *is startled. The phone makes up her mind. As it rings again, she moves toward it* . . . *Blocking* CANTRY's *path*.) Please, Miss Cantry! (*The phone rings again*)

CANTRY. (*Shaking*) Let me go by, Frances. (*As the phone rings again*, FRAN, *horrified, moves out of her way*. CANTRY *goes to telephone. She speaks into it:*) Hello . . . Mr. Eldridge? . . . Yes, I'll speak to him.

THE LIGHTS ON THE OFFICE FADE QUICKLY

END OF ACT II

ACT III

Scene 1

Two areas of the stage are lighted—

The Bedroom and the Main Hall

It is some minutes after the end of the previous scene. The bedroom is empty. SELMA KEENEY *stands by the small desk in the main hallway. She extracts a recording from a record album and plays it on the portable victrola. It is a Handel oratorio . . . As the music plays, the door to the bedroom opens and* PATTY *enters. Spent and harried, she leans against the door for a moment's respite. Recovered somewhat, she recalls what she has come upstairs for: she has been, and still is, looking for* LEE.

PATTY. Lee . . .? (*She slips down onto the bed and sits there, staring vacantly ahead of her. She forces herself back to awareness and starts slowly out of the room again . . . Meanwhile, downstairs,* SELMA KEENEY *hums a phrase of the oratorio, trying to commit it to memory. The outside door opens and* FRAN *enters hurriedly. She wears no coat or hat and her hair is disheveled; she has been walking fast.* SELMA *sees her and stiffens*)

FRAN. Selma, have you seen Lee anywhere? (*Without a word* SELMA *turns on her heel and walks outdoors.* FRAN *looks after her, humiliated and grimly amused at this token that she, as well as her sister, is in disgrace.* PATTY *comes down the stairs*) Did you find her?

PATTY. (*Tonelessly*) No. She's not up there.

FRAN. I've looked all over the campus . . . Patty, when Miss Cantry dismissed everyone from the office . . . did you see where Lee went?

PATTY. (*Desperately*) No . . . Oh, Fran, she's the only one who can help us! And she will, I know! I'm sure she's not in with Dru . . . I'm sure of it!

FRAN. Of course she's not. (*Suddenly there is a chorus of chatter and laughter and* SYLVIA, MATHILDA *and* SALLY *run into the room. They are in hockey clothes.* SYLVIA *and* SALLY *see* FRAN *and* PATTY *and their chatter ceases. But* MATHILDA, *who hasn't noticed them, goes to the table and looks around, as if searching for something. Then in a boisterous voice:*)

MATHILDA. Hey, who snitched my hockey stick? Did anybody swipe my hockey—! (*In turning, she comes face to face with* PATTY—*and her words stop in mid sentence. A painful pause.* FRAN *breaks it:*)

FRAN. (*Quietly*) Your hockey stick is under the table. (*The stillness takes hold again*) Come on, Patty, let's go to your room. (*They slip away from the group, up the stairs*)

MATHILDA. Oh, what a boner! I could bite my tongue off!

SYLVIA. Why? I'm glad she heard it! It couldn't have been neater if you'd said it on purpose!

MATHILDA. I don't believe Patty's the kind to do such things! (*Starting for the stairs*) And I'm going to tell her I wasn't making cracks at her—

SALLY. Don't be a moron! They're leaving here—but you're staying. If it gets around you were friendly with them—you'll buy yourself a pack of grief. MATHILDA *comes down off the landing*) Anyway—did you see her face?—she's as guilty as Judas!

MATHILDA. (*Weakly*) I don't know . . .

SYLVIA. (*Swinging the hockey stick*) Come on! Hock-eeeeeeee! (*With a concerted rush they are out of the room . . .* PATTY *and* FRAN *enter the bedroom.* PATTY *sits in the chair and* FRAN *stands by the window, toying with the blind. Neither speaks. At last:*)

PATTY. Fran—what are we to do?

FRAN. I don't know. (*Another silence. Suddenly the door opens and* LEE *stands there, her face full of self-recrimination and unhappiness.* FRAN *turns quickly from the window and* PATTY *jumps up*)

PATTY. Lee, where were you? We've been looking all over for you.

LEE. (*With difficulty*) I tried to get away from everybody. I went up to the third floor fire escape—I just sat on the steps . . . (*Then, irrelevantly*) It's getting cold out . . .

FRAN. Lee, you've got to tell us what happened? How did you get mixed up in this?

LEE. (*Miserably*) What's the good of talking and talking?

FRAN. (*Quietly*) Lee . . . Patty is your friend; she's my sister. She's accused of being a thief. Do we let that go without saying a word? You don't believe Patty stole those things, do you?

LEE. (*Hopelessly*) A lot of difference it makes what I believe.

PATTY. It makes a difference to me.

LEE. All right—I don't believe you're a thief! I didn't believe it before—I don't believe it now—I'll never believe it! There!—I'm a great big help to you!

FRAN. (*Quietly*) Then, if you don't believe it, I can't understand how you could lie about that box.

LEE. I didn't lie! I discovered the box—I discovered the things in it!

FRAN. Was Dru in the room when you searched Patty's bureau?

LEE. Yes . . . I knew the stolen things couldn't be there—but they were there! I didn't want them to be—but they were! (*She starts to tremble*)

FRAN. (*Keeping a tight hold on herself*) Lee, why has this hit *you* so hard? Because you've lost faith in Patty? Because you secretly believe Patty did steal . . .?

LEE. No.

FRAN. Then why?

LEE. Because I helped Dru—and I loathe myself for it! I was on Dru's side—against the first real friend I ever had!

PATTY. If you discovered the box you couldn't do anything else.

LEE. I could have lied when they asked me! I *should* have lied! In this case, a lie would have been the truth! It was only a little question of fact—and what have facts got to do with what I know in my heart!

PATTY. (*On the verge of tears*) Lee . . . thank you.

LEE. For what? For something I *should* have done for you? (*A pause.* PATTY *collects herself*)

FRAN. Lee—when you discovered the box, why didn't you come to me immediately? Or even to Patty? Before all this came out in the open—why didn't you let us know?

LEE. I couldn't . . .

FRAN. Why couldn't you?

LEE. (*Desperately*) Oh, for God's sake—can't you imagine why?

FRAN. I see . . . Dru threatened you.

LEE. Yes.

FRAN. Lee, I know you want to help Patty. Will you do as I tell you?

97

LEE. Of course!

FRAN. I want you to go to Miss Cantry—tell her Dru bullied you
—as she bullies so many others—

LEE. (*Getting herself under control*) What good is it, Miss Morritt? We're just snatching at straws!

FRAN. —tell her this is all mixed up with your being Jewish—

LEE. (*She looks at* FRAN *suddenly. She straightens*) . . . You
say that to me now? Why didn't you say so the instant you
read my paper?—or even this afternoon when I asked you!
One word from you—a single word—and I'd have marched into
Miss Cantry's office. Why didn't you say it?! (FRAN *is silent.* LEE
continues with deadly calm) Why didn't you tell me that by
pretending not to be Jewish I played right into Dru's hands?!

FRAN. (*Shaken*) I was wrong—I didn't know—

LEE. Oh, yes, you did know! You didn't want to get into an un-
tidy situation! But now that you *are* in it, you want me to be
brave—for *you!* Miss Morritt, why aren't you brave for yourself?!

PATTY. Lee—please—

LEE. It's true, Patty! Ask your sister how often she's ducked out
of a fight! (*To* FRAN) When you came into that meeting about
the Vidge I thought you were riding a white horse! But then
you played it safe—you talked about procedure! And when *I*
needed you, you played it safe a second time! (*Then very
quietly*) And you know what, Miss Morritt? I suspect there was
a third time—and it had to do with Emmy.

FRAN. (*With a start*) You don't know what you're talking about!

LEE. I don't know—I only guess. And my guess tells me there
was dirty work!

PATTY. Lee! I don't like you talking like that!

LEE. Ask her how Emmy got wound up in this. Miss Cantry hinted that your sister knows something about it. Ask her.

PATTY. Stop it, Lee!

LEE. (*Quietly*) All right, we'll let it go. (*Silence*) Well . . . I *am* going to Miss Cantry. I'm going to tell her I'm Jewish . . . Patty, your sister thinks that'll help you. I don't. Anyway, I'm not doing it for you. I wish I *could* do something for you, Pat . . . I wish I could. (LEE *departs quietly . . . From downstairs, the oratorio music swells and fades . . . then . . .*)

PATTY. (*At the window*) It must be getting late—Helen and Amy Butler are coming back from the movies . . . We were supposed to meet them there . . . (*With an intake of breath*) Oh, Fran— everything's so wrong—everything's dirty . . . (*She goes to pieces, weeping*)

FRAN. Don't, Patty.

PATTY. Even you and I—something's happened—

FRAN. Patty, please . . .

PATTY. (*Collecting herself*) What do we do? . . . start packing?

FRAN. Let's wait a bit . . .

PATTY. . . . I wish I hadn't been so angry with Lee—she's a good person—I shouldn't have been! But she was hinting those awful things about you and Emmy. (FRAN *moves away*) Fran—you don't know anything about Emmy, do you? (*Then quickly*) I'm sorry, I shouldn't have asked that. (*A long silence. Slowly, watching* FRAN *closely,* PATTY *is filled with dread*) Fran . . .?

FRAN. Yes?

PATTY. What did she mean about Emmy?

FRAN. (*Nervously*) I don't know.

99

PATTY. (*Quietly*) How did Emmy get mixed up in this? Fran, maybe—! Did Emmy steal those things?

FRAN. No, she didn't.

PATTY. But Miss Cantry said she confessed to—?

FRAN. She didn't confess anything.

PATTY. You mean Miss Cantry was lying?

FRAN. Yes.

PATTY. But why—I don't understand—?

FRAN. (*Tormented*) Miss Cantry discharged her. Emmy didn't know she was being discharged for stealing!

PATTY. (*It reaches her with the impact of a blow*) Oh, no!

FRAN. (*Quickly*) Miss Cantry had to do it! She was desperate—it meant the school—it meant everything—she had to do it!

PATTY. (*A pause.* PATTY *cannot bring herself to ask the next question. At last:*) Fran . . . were you there when Emmy was discharged?

FRAN. I had nothing to do with it!

PATTY. Were you there?

FRAN. Yes.

PATTY. And you didn't tell Emmy what was happening?

FRAN. It was out of my hands—I couldn't!

PATTY. And then—when Emmy left the room—You didn't stop Cantry? You didn't kill her?!

FRAN. Patty, you don't kill people!

PATTY. And when the girls came into the room, you didn't shout the truth? You just stood there?—You didn't say anything? You let Cantry blame that innocent woman!

FRAN. Stop it—let me alone!

PATTY. Lee was right—it was some kind of arrangement . . . (*Then with ferocious intensity*) What did you *get* out of it?

FRAN. (*Agonized*) Don't talk as if I were bribed!

PATTY. You did to Emmy exactly what Dru is doing to me! *What did you get out of it!!*

FRAN. (*With an outcry of self-denunciation*) All right—it's true! I've worked hand-in-glove with them! I didn't *want* to, but I did! I hadn't the guts to fight them—so I joined them!

PATTY. (*Horrified*) Yes . . . You did.

FRAN. (*Seeing* PATTY'S *revulsion,* FRAN *pleads*) Patty, listen—(*But* PATTY *retreats toward the door*) Everything's so black and white to you! No compromise—no quarter! You're all justice and no understanding! I did it for Cantry—yes!—because I was fond of her—because I felt sorry for her! I did it so we could stay on here —for you and me—

PATTY. Don't say that! Don't say you did it for me!

FRAN. For both of us! (*She reaches out for* PATTY *who pulls away as though revolted by contact with her*)

PATTY. Don't ever touch me! (*She flies out of the room*)

FRAN. Patty—Patty—(FRAN *keeps calling* PATTY'S *name. She stands there holding the door, swinging it a little and crying aloud*)

THE LIGHTS FADE

ACT III

Scene 2

Quickly, sharp and full, the lights come up—on—

The Main Hallway and the Office

A few minutes after the preceding scene . . . The music is coming to a close . . . In the office, MISS CANTRY *is seated, her elbows on the desk, her head in her hands; immobilized. At last she raises her head, sighs deeply and rises heavily from her chair. Despondent and aimless, she walks about the room.* LAURA *enters.*

LAURA. I told Selma and Dru to come down and claim their property.

CANTRY. How about Abby?

LAURA. She's away for the week-end.

CANTRY. (*Spiritlessly*) See that she comes for her fraternity pin Monday morning.

LAURA. Yes, I will. (*She looks at her watch*) It's dinner time, Auntie Sara. (CANTRY *doesn't answer*) You'll have a headache if you go without your dinner.

CANTRY. Never mind . . . never mind.

LAURA. I don't know why you worry yourself over them. After what Patricia's done—good riddance to both of them!

CANTRY. Please, Laura.

LAURA. (*After a moment*) Do you want me to go through this room and get Miss Morritt's things together?

CANTRY. (*Tormented*) For heaven's sake—can't you do these things without asking questions!

LAURA. (*Meekly*) Yes, Auntie Sara. (LAURA *goes to work assembling* FRAN'S *effects.* CANTRY *stands at the window, depressedly looking out at the gathering darkness . . . Meanwhile, as though in panic,* NANCY *enters the Main Hall from outdoors. Simultaneously,* DRU *is coming down the stairs.* DRU *spies* NANCY *just as the latter starts for the office door. Quickly,* DRU *walks to her, blocking* NANCY'S *way*)

DRU. Nancy, where are you going?

NANCY. I—I've got to see Miss Cantry—

DRU. Why? What for?

NANCY. (*Disconnectedly*) About Patty—I've got to talk to Miss Cantry—

DRU. (*Desperately*) Listen, don't spoil things!

NANCY. But I'm scared!

DRU. Everythings over—it's settled. Just stay close to me until Patty and Miss Morritt leave the school—and everything will be fine. (*Then more gently*) Take my word for it, it will! I'll see that you have friends, Nancy—I'll get you dates—you can come home with me for week-ends. (*During the last speech,* LAURA *has finished her work at the desk. She has left the office and now appears in the hallway. Simultaneously,* SELMA *comes in from outdoors*)

LAURA. Dru, I told you Miss Cantry wants to see you. You, too, Selma.

SELMA. Yes, I'm going. (*She goes up to the office door and knocks as* LAURA *departs*)

CANTRY. Come in.

DRU. (*Quietly to* NANCY) Now stay with me, Nancy. Don't get out of my sight. Come on. (SELMA *has entered the office.* DRU *and* NANCY *now follow*)

CANTRY. Come in, girls . . . Now that this terrible incident is over, I want it forgotten quickly. Do you understand?

SELMA. Yes.

DRU. Of course, Miss Cantry.

CANTRY. In the confusion that went on here a while ago, I neglected to return your property. Selma, here is your pen—and your money, Dru.

SELMA. Thank you. (SELMA *leaves*)

DRU. Thank you—very much.

DRU. (*With elaborate sentimentality*) Miss Cantry, I want to tell you how sorry I am all this happened. But you know, in a way it's a good thing it all came out.

CANTRY. (*With weary distaste*) Please, Dru.

DRU. But it is a good thing, Miss Cantry. It shows you the people you can rely on.

CANTRY. Dru, I don't want to talk about it—not now.

DRU. Yes . . . I understand. (DRU *and* NANCY *start out as the door opens and* PATTY *enters.* PATTY *and* DRU *confront each other for a split second, then* DRU *and* NANCY *depart*)

PATTY. Miss Cantry—

CANTRY. I don't know what you're doing here, Patricia. You should be in your room packing.

PATTY. I don't want to stay here any longer than necessary, but—

CANTRY. (*Interrupting*) It's not necessary that you stay at all.

You don't seem to understand, Patricia—your sister is dismissed and you are expelled.

PATTY. But you can't send me away without a chance to clear myself. I can't just leave this thing behind me—

CANTRY. (*Forcing herself to say this*) You should have thought of that sooner.

PATTY. (*Throwing herself on* CANTRY's *mercy*) Miss Cantry, look at me! You've worked with girls for so many years, you must have some way of telling whether a girl's a thief. After forty years, your heart should tell you!

CANTRY. It's not as easy as that. My heart doesn't tell me the truth about these things. (FRAN *has entered. She hears this and speaks quietly:*)

FRAN. Then you're a person of bad heart.

CANTRY. (*With an outcry*) Frances, why did you come in here again! Why didn't you just go! Why make things more painful for both of us!

FRAN. Miss Cantry, I wouldn't have come in here if I thought you really believed my sister a thief.

CANTRY. I have to believe it!

FRAN. But *do* you believe it? Do you?

CANTRY. Yes! . . . Frances, do you think this is easy for me? Do you think I *want* you to leave—?

FRAN. (*Quietly*) Just a moment, Miss Cantry. I'm not leaving.

CANTRY. Not leaving . . .?

FRAN. I'm going to stay here until my sister is free of disgrace. (PATTY, *stunned, makes a quick move toward her*) And if you try to get me out, a lot of people will learn what goes on in this school!

CANTRY. Yes—you can do us a lot of harm. But you realize what harm you can do to yourself?

FRAN. I'll take my chances.

CANTRY. If there should be a scandal, you'll be part of it. You won't be able to get a position. Frances—I beg you—for your own good—leave the school quietly!

FRAN. You mean sneak out, Miss Cantry? No . . . I'm not playing it safe anymore. (*At this instant, a commotion outside the office.* LEE's *voice is heard, excitedly:*)

LEE'S VOICE. Patty! Miss Morritt!

PATTY. We're in here, Lee! (LEE *comes racing into the room. She is followed by* SELMA *and* NANCY, *and* DRU *is there too—frightened—trying to restrain* LEE)

LEE. Miss Morritt—! I just thought of something—! I don't know why we didn't think of it before—! (*She crosses to* CANTRY *excitedly*) Miss Cantry, when Selma lost her fountain pen—Patty hadn't even arrived here at school! Patty couldn't possibly have taken it—she wasn't here! (*A quick motion in the room*)

PATTY. That's right! I was in my room no more than fifteen minutes when Mil told Dru about the pen!

FRAN. How do you explain that, Dru?

DRU. I don't have to explain anything! (*To* PATTY) You arrived ahead of me—that's all I know! And Selma's pen had already been stolen! (*To* CANTRY—*indicating* PATTY *and* LEE) Miss Cantry, look at them—they got together and dreamed this story up! you're not going to believe *them*, are you? (*Pointing to* PATTY) That one's a thief—(*Pointing to* LEE)—and that one—

LEE. Wait! Let me say it! (*With quiet strength*) Miss Cantry, I'm Jewish.

CANTRY. You're—? But you told me—?

DRU. She lied! (*To* LEE) You lied to get into the school—and you're lying now! (*To* CANTRY) She ought to be expelled with the other two!

FRAN. (*Grimly*) We're being expelled for theft—what's she being expelled for?

CANTRY. (*Quickly*) She's not being expelled for anything! I will not have this matter twisted into an issue of intolerance! I have no personal feeling against Jews—

DRU. How about liars?

CANTRY. (*Angrily*) Drucilla! I don't want to talk about it!

DRU. You were quite willing to talk about Jews to my father! Many's the time he stood by you in those board meetings because you promised him—

CANTRY. That's not true! (*In an outburst*) Enough of this! (*Dismissing* SELMA . . . *To the others, as* SELMA *leaves*) Let's put an end to it! There'll always be ifs and supposes and a thousand lame alibis!

FRAN. Not one bit as lame as the case against my sister!

CANTRY. The case against your sister stands on the testimony of her friends! Lee discovered the box and Nancy saw her with the fountain pen!

FRAN. (*Turning quickly to* NANCY) Nancy, *did* you see her with that pen? Maybe you saw her holding something else? Maybe it was dark in there—

NANCY. Oh no, it was quite light—the middle of the morning—

PATTY. The middle of the morning? What time?

NANCY. About eleven o'clock.

PATTY. I was in chemistry lab from ten to twelve!

THE YOUNG AND FAIR

NANCY. (*Unevenly*) I—I don't know . . . It might have been earlier. . . .

PATTY. Nancy, it might have been somebody else you saw!

FRAN. (*Suddenly*) Good heavens!—maybe you didn't see *anybody* with that pen!

NANCY. I did!—I did!

FRAN. (*Going to* NANCY, *gently*) Nancy, you've made a mistake, haven't you?

DRU. Let her alone!

FRAN. Nancy, listen—

NANCY. Don't question me—please don't question me!

FRAN. Nancy, don't be afraid—nobody's going to hurt you. You were in the infirmary, weren't you? Did you leave it without anybody knowing?

PATTY. Nancy, who do you think took those things? Did you take them?

DRU. She's trying to trap Nancy—it's a dirty trick!

FRAN. Stay out of this! (*To* NANCY) Go on, Nancy—did you take them?

NANCY. (*Simply, naively*) Yes . . . I intended to give them back, honest I did. But everybody got me so confused . . . (*Vacantly*) Are you trying to get me confused, Miss Morritt?

DRU. Yes, she is! Don't say any more, Nancy!

FRAN. I told you to be quiet!

PATTY. Go on, Nancy—just tell us whatever you want to.

NANCY. (*Disjointedly*) Yes, I took them. Sometimes I don't know why I do these things . . . and sometimes it's so clear.

FRAN. Go on.

NANCY. (*She tells this as a child might tell a fairy story—with wonder and sweetness. However from time to time there is a small burst of fear or anger, and this gives the entire telling a quality that is both pathetic and unwholesome*) I never wanted to come away to school. My mother made me. She's always making me do things—so I won't mope around the house. She doesn't like me to be different from other girls. When I'm different she's ashamed—because—because—(*Lamely, with hurt bewilderment —as though she has lost her place*) I don't know why. Oh, yes, I do. (*Happily, for she has momentarily recaptured her thoughts*) Because we're a very superior family. (*This last she has learned by rote. She says it with the pride she has copied from her mother's voice*) When I got to the school, I—I wanted to get away from the girls . . . I had a headache—But my mother wouldn't want me to hide from the others and be a coward . . . Am I a coward, Miss . . . Miss . . .? (*She cannot remember* FRAN's *name*)

FRAN. No, Nancy.

NANCY. No. I'm just like the other girls. I want to say what they say and have what they have . . . I'm jealous if I can't do that! (*With a low surge of anger*) So jealous that I want to *do* something to them!—take their *things!*—do *something!* (*Then blandly*) It takes a lot of courage to steal—a lot of courage. Cowards can't steal . . . Really, I would have given all those things back. When the other girls got to like me—really—(*Then, anger again*) But they'd have to like me!

FRAN. Nancy . . . after you took the things, what did you do?

NANCY. There was so much trouble I didn't want to have them any more. I didn't know what to do. (*Looking at* DRU) So she promised to help me.

DRU. I had nothing to do with it!

NANCY. (*Gently*) Oh, yes, you did. Didn't you tell me to put the things in Patty's stationery box? (FRAN *turns away from* NANCY *and confronts* DRU)

DRU. (*Deliberately*) Miss Cantry, that girl's out of her mind!

NANCY. (*In a wild outburst*) No! I'm not! I'm not!

DRU. Look at her—she's insane!

NANCY. Don't say that!—I'll kill you!—don't say that! (*With which* NANCY *flies across the room and reaches for* DRU's *throat.* DRU *struggles as the others try to separate them*)

FRAN. Nancy, stop it—stop it!

CANTRY. Don't! Please! Let her alone!   }   TOGETHER

PATTY. Nancy! Please, Nancy!

(THEY *separate them.* DRU, *breathless, subsides on the couch*)

NANCY. (*Her collapse is complete now. The weak bonds that tied her to reason have given way. She weeps, to* FRAN:) You made me tell everything. My head aches. What will they tell my mother? My head hurts me—

FRAN. Nancy, we'll go up to the infirmary. Come on, Nancy. (*She puts her arm around* NANCY's *shoulder*)

NANCY. My head aches—

FRAN. Please—come with me.

NANCY. You made me tell! Take your hands off me! I won't go with you! (*She darts quickly away from* FRAN)

LEE. (*Stepping forward*) Then come with me. Come on, Nancy.

NANCY. Yes . . . My mother's going to find out about it! I'll get arrested! (*She keeps wailing forlornly as* LEE *repeats soothingly:*)

LEE. It's all right, Nancy—don't worry—don't worry—(*By now,* LEE *has* NANCY *out of the room*)

CANTRY. (*After a moment*) That poor child . . . She'll have to be sent home . . .

FRAN. (*With a mirthless smile*) Maybe Mrs. Gear will give you a gift . . . for a special service.

CANTRY. Patricia, I've done you a terrible wrong. If I can ever make it up to you—

PATTY. (*Coldly*) You can't make anything up to me!

CANTRY. Please—bear with me! (*Disorganizedly*) I'm not equal to my burden any more—what will I say to the school—to Mrs. Gear—?

FRAN. (*Quietly*) Might I suggest the truth, Miss Cantry?

CANTRY. The truth will treat me cruelly, Frances! And you, too!

FRAN. We've done cruel things.

CANTRY. (*Crying out*) From fear—can't you understand it—from fear!

FRAN. Is that supposed to excuse us?

CANTRY. If there's no excuse for us, Frances—then the whole frightened world is guilty!

FRAN. (*Gently*) Miss Cantry—I'm not judging you. Only myself.

CANTRY. If I'm to be judged—I've accomplished some good in my life! I've built a fine school.

FRAN. (*Breaking out*) Oh, no! That's what you *set out* to build! But look at it—it's ridden with viciousness and hatred and—

CANTRY. Please, Frances—

FRAN. This school is a plague spot! Is this what you set out to build?

CANTRY. (*Collapsing*) No . . . I dreamed something quite different . . . (*Then in great despair*) I worked—I indulged myself in nothing. I did whatever was demanded of me—however hateful—

FRAN. (*Quietly*) That's just it . . . it was killed by the very mischief you hoped would save it.

CANTRY. It's not killed yet! I won't believe it! (*Then suddenly*) Frances, stay on here! We can reclaim this place—you and I—

FRAN. Do you really want to reclaim it? Or do you simply want to be secure in the school—just as it is?

CANTRY. Show me what to do!

FRAN. Make a clean sweep, Miss Cantry! Start by reinstating Emmy—

CANTRY. Yes—yes—

FRAN. Remove all restrictions—

CANTRY. It'll be done—I promise you—!

FRAN. And most important . . . You'd have to expel Dru Eldridge!

DRU. Miss Cantry, you wouldn't do that!

FRAN. Did you expect to get away with everything you've done, Dru?

DRU. (*Quickly to* CANTRY) Miss Cantry, you've got a choice to make. It's Miss Morritt or me. If you expel me, there'll be somebody else in your chair! You'll have nothing but Miss Morritt and her pipe dream!

CANTRY. (*Apprehensively*) Frances—we *can* do it—can't we—?

FRAN. I'm not saying it'll be easy. It won't. But if we work together—(*Pleading*) Miss Cantry, I'll work so hard with you—!

CANTRY. It would mean beginning all over—with nothing—

FRAN. With a blackboard in a dining room—! But wasn't it better then?—Weren't you happier?

DRU. (*Relentlessly*) That was how many years ago, Miss Cantry? How old were you then? How old are you now?

FRAN. (*Desperately—to* DRU) Why don't you give her a chance? (*Silence*)

FRAN. Well, Miss Cantry?

CANTRY. (*Suddenly letting everything fall away*) . . . Dreams are for the young.

FRAN. Don't say that—please—!

CANTRY. (*With a bitter smile*) No . . . It was a long thought, Frances. But I'm afraid I haven't time . . .

DRU. Well—goodbye, Miss Morritt! (*She pulls herself to her full height and with a smile, walks out*)

PATTY. Miss Cantry, if you let Dru get away with all she's done, the Eldridges will take you over completely!

CANTRY. (*Looking away*) Maybe it will be a relief . . . When I was as young as you, I thought free choice was a blessing of God. But now I know it's a trick to make us struggle. A bitter, bitter struggle—without peace, without comfort . . . And now I'm very tired . . . (*She looks at* PATTY *and half smiles*) In time you'll know what I'm talking about . . .

PATTY. (*Quietly*) Before I do, I hope I'll be dead. (*Quietly she leaves the room.* FRAN *starts to follow her*)

CANTRY. Frances, wait! Don't leave me. You'll have a good position here—a place of security—

FRAN. A hiding-place! That's what I came here for. But there isn't any hiding-place!

CANTRY. What will you do with yourself? Remember you had difficulty getting a job—

FRAN. Oh, no! I had difficulty getting a genteel job for a genteel lady! But now I'm just an ordinary woman!

CANTRY. I hate to think what might happen to you.

FRAN. I don't know what will happen to me if I leave—but that doesn't frighten me any more. However, I do know what will happen if I stay—and that terrifies me.

CANTRY. What will happen, Frances?

FRAN. (*Gently*) I'll become like you . . . Goodbye, Miss Cantry. (*She goes out. And with her departure, the last vestige of vitality forsakes* CANTRY. *She looks at the emptiness that surrounds her and slowly sits down at her desk. Gently, she buries her head in her arms as the lights dim on the office and go up on the Main Hall.* PATTY *is there, sitting on the bench, as* FRAN *enters from the office and* LEE *enters from outdoors*)

LEE. I have to pack. I'm going home.

FRAN. I guess we'll all be leaving soon. (*A moment; then*) Lee, I want to thank you for what you said to me before. I feel as though you'd seen me through an illness.

LEE. Sooner or later you'd have seen yourself through.

PATTY. I'd better start packing, too. You'll wait for us, won't you, Lee?

LEE. (*Embracing* PATTY) Of course. (*She starts up the steps and stops. With new-found serenity*) You know, I arrived here alone. It's wonderful to think we'll all be leaving together. (*Quickly she goes upstairs . . . A moment, then:*)

PATTY. It's strange . . . I've been here only a week . . . but I feel so much older.

FRAN. And I feel younger!

PATTY. Another week like this and we'd be twins!

FRAN. Yes . . . (*They look at one another and smile*) There's a newness about me—everything new! It's like being—

PATTY. Happy Birthday, Fran! (*She extends her hand.* FRAN, *deeply moved, takes it*)

CURTAIN

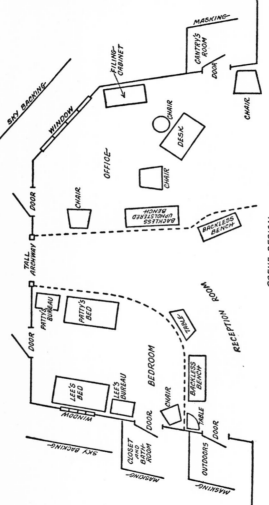

SCENE DESIGN

"THE YOUNG AND FAIR"

Simplified Floor Plan for "The Young and Fair"

Dotted lines indicate wall partitions high enough
to designate room divisions but not so high as to
obscure sight lines. No higher than twenty inches.